Legal Balm

Everyday Law for Everybody

First Edition	2010
Reprint	**2016**

Legal Balm

Everyday Law for Everybody

Ravi Sodhi
Advocate
Punjab & Haryana High Court
Addl. Standing Counsel, Chandigarh Administration
(Former Addl., Advocate General, Punjab)

Universal
Law Publishing
an imprint of LexisNexis

LexisNexis®

This book is a publication of **LexisNexis®**
(A Division of Reed Elsevier India (Pvt) Ltd)
14th floor, Building No 10, Tower–B, DLF Cyber City, Phase-II,
Gurgaon–122002, Haryana, India.
Tel : + 91 124 4774444 Fax: + 91 124 4774100

Website : www.lexisnexis.co.in / E-mail : help.in@lexisnexis.com

---

Ravi Sodhi : *Legal Balm, Everyday Law for Everybody,* First Edition, Reprint 2016

ISBN: 978-81-7534-897-4

Printed by: Sanat Printers,

Printed and bound in India.

"This book has been digitally reprinted on Print on Demand services by Sanat Printers, Haryana. The contents remains same, however, the quality of paper, printing and binding is identical, but not as perfect as the original printing."

G.S. Singhvi
Judge
Supreme Court of India

4, Motilal Nehru Marg,
New Delhi-110 011

FOREWORD

In his work titled '... Legal Balm', Shri Ravi Sodhi has touched upon subjects which are extremely relevant to the contemporary society. He has made in-depth analysis of various topics relating to constitutionalism and changing values in the field of human rights, accountability of citizens and pointed out acute deficiencies in the working of three pillars of democracy *i.e.,* legislature, executive and judiciary. The scientific division of various Chapters is bound to attract attention of different segments of the society because the author has made an attempt to bring to the fore malise which has afflicted our institutions. Shri Sodhi's treatment to various subjects shows his deep concern about the wrongs being done to have-nots of the society and failure of justice delivery system to protect weaker segments of the society. One cannot but appreciate concern shown by the author on the issue of huge pendency of the cases which has adversely affected the image of the justice delivery system in general and the courts in particular. I am sure the book will be useful to the lawyers, judges, teachers, law students, social scientists and all those who are interested in the democratic values and human rights.

(G.S. Singhvi)

Dr. Kiran Bedi
INDIAN POLICE SERVICE

Office Add.
56, Basement, Uday Park
New Delhi – 110049 (INDIA)
Tel.: +91-11-47100700

MESSAGE

"Legal Balm" should actually have been named "Legal Bomb" for its path breaking, innovative concepts and solutions for the ever so needed accountability in our public life.

The Jurist in Ravi Sodhi has suggested tailor made legal solutions for various problems confronting all of us in India. With more than a decade as a single man free legal aid through the columns of Indian Express and Hindustan Times (Chandigarh Editions), Mr. Sodhi has sufficient credentials and exposure for contributing to the cause of Nation Building. I congratulate him and wish him the best for effective application of his Special Balm-The Legal Balm.

(KIRAN BEDI)

NALSAR University of Law, Hyderabad

National Academy of Legal Studies and Research University
Justice City, Shameerpet, R.R. District, Hyderabad - 500 078. A P., India
Ph.: Off: 91-40-23498102 Res: +91-8418-245155 Fax: +91-8418-245161

Prof. (Dr.) Veer Singh
Vice Chancellor

The Theory of Constitutional Tort advocated by the author reflects a practical everyday solution for everybody after the R.T.I. Act for the major ill of lack of accountability in our systems which are on oxygen. The broad spectrum of topics covered in a simple but powerful manner is socially most relevant today. This is specifically true for the pragmatic solutions for the docket crisis, modernization of the Judicial systems, tackling accidental fatalities and Police atrocities. The truth serum for Injecting the Judicial process with truthfulness is of paramount importance. The work is original and outstanding.

Singh. 21/1/2010

(VEER SINGH)

Department of Laws
Panjab University, Chandigarh
(Established under the Panjab University Act VII of 1947)
Phone: 2541577, Fax: 2540381, Intercom 4161 (Chairman) Office-4157-58
Email: lawsdept@pa.ac.in;lawlib@pu.ac.in

No. 357/N/Law Date 25-2-2010

MESSAGE

Law is an instrument of social change. It must keep pace and should continue to re-modulate itself in commensurate with socio-economic changes. Law is a means to an end and not an end in itself. It must act as a catalyst to meet the new challenges of the society from time to time. If the law fails to respond to the demands of the society then the very purpose of law shall be defeated.

"Legal Balm" is indeed a complete jurisprudential recipe for disaster prevention of the country's deteriorating systems. The concept of providing Constitutional Tort a constitutional status through appropriate legislation would be a path breaking measure for promoting the accountability audit.

The original and practical suggestions for tuning in our law to the prevailing conditions, when implemented, would go, a long way in providing a long needed relief to the common man. The broad spectrum of topics covered are most relevant specially the portion relating to speedy justice, ensuring safe roads, using technology for updating and streamlining systems, etc. The book is an appropriate example of creativity and out of the box thinking. I wish Mr. Ravi Sodhi all the best.

Dr. Paramjit S. Jaswal
Professor & Chairman

Preface

Lack of accountability is the basic malaise which is threatening our self esteem and sense of social justice. (Recent example of **unarmed helpless citizens demanding clean drinking water in Bombay being mercilessly beaten and one of them losing his life for water is a slur on the Indian System and an example of the agony a citizen has to undergo for the mere procurement of drinking water. One is reminded of the famous remark of a visionary. "Water, water, everywhere not a drop to drink."** There have been judicially noticed examples in cases like *Khatri* v. *State of Bihar,* AIR 1981 SC 928 where prisoners have been blinded). Thus accountability is a major national issue with us. **Rightly has it been remarked that an hour of justice is worth a hundred of prayers.** Revival of public justice should be our foremost national priority. Regrettably, we have not grappled with our problems at a deeper level. Our approach at solving national problems has been casual, superficial and cosmetic. **We yet have not been able make a tangible headway because we have tried to cure the fever by cooling the thermometer.**

Legally, the Law of Torts and more so, the concept of **Constitutional Tort** as an instrument of accountability has been totally ignored. The consequences have been disastrous and are there for all of us to see. In my humble effort, I have tried to revive the national spirit by resurrecting the concept of Constitutional Tort. This book also includes daily issues of docket crisis, truth in court proceedings, witness protection, police excesses, accidental deaths, computerization of judicial system and E - Courts, Cyber laws, Issues of Handicapped, The jury system, etc. . . . One feels that most of us are living a life of emptiness, indifference and cynicism because of generalized inefficiency and complacency. I, for one feel strongly with Norman Cousins that **the great tragedy of life is not death. The tragedy of life is allowing the inside of us to die while we still live.**

Every day, we find thousands of persons dying due to callous and avoidable Road accidents. These routine tickets to the morgue have also not been able to move us into constructive action. We have become more of **'wandering generalities'** rather than **'meaningful specifics'**. We, as a nation need to readjust our sensitivity thresholds. **We need to become more meaningful in our individual lives and realize that though each one of us cannot write great novels but definitely each one of us can live them. Indeed, one of our foremost tasks is to give birth to ourselves in the form of individual improvements which in turn would result in improvements of the systems in the country.** Everyone's parameters for success are different. I, for one, would subscribe to **'Ralph Waldo Emersons' Recipe for success**. It reads thus:

> "To laugh often and much; to win the respect of intelligent people and the affection of children; to earn the appreciation of honest critics and endure the betrayal of false friends; to appreciate beauty, to find the best in others; to leave the world a bit better, whether by a healthy child, a garden patch or a redeemed social condition; to know even one life has breathed easier because you have lived. This is to have succeeded".

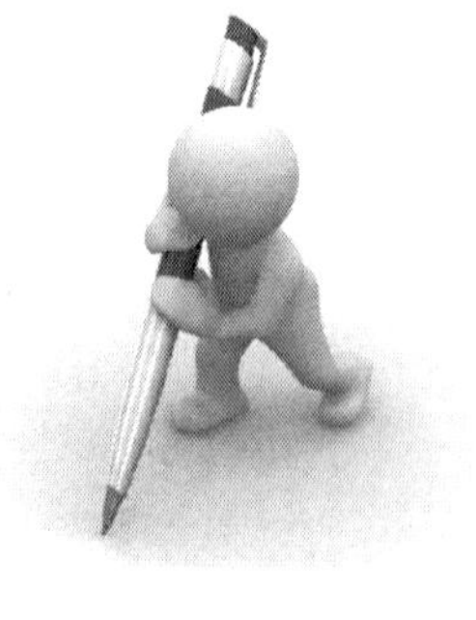

Thanksgiving

My Special thanks to Dr. H.K. Bali (Fortis – Mohali) and Dr. Parveen Kumar (PGI Chandigarh) for encouraging me and constantly reminding me to undertake writing this challenging book project. Last but not the least, my gratitude to my co-workers and more of friends Mr. Himanshu Verma (Panchkula) and Mr. Shashi Bhushan Goyal (Panchkula) who provided immense support, without which, the completion of this book would not have been possible.

CONTENTS

TABLE OF CASES

LET US HUMANIZE JUSTICE

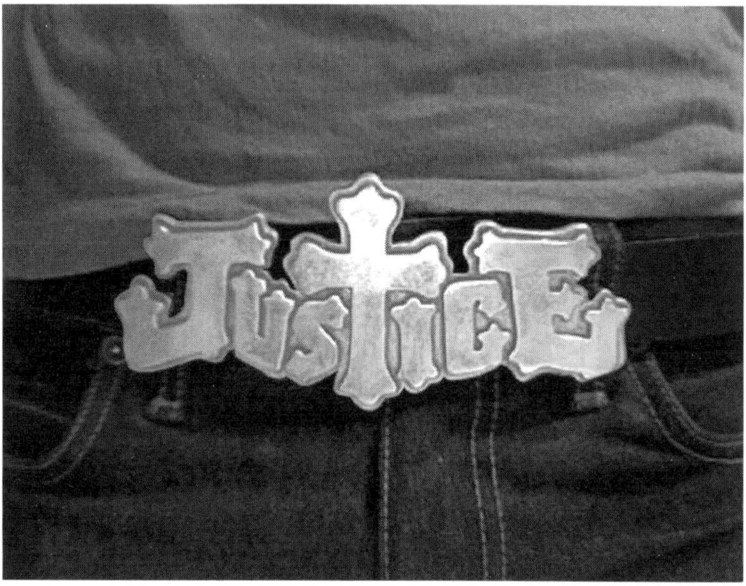

"Morality cannot be legislated,
But behavior can be regulated.
Judicial decrees may not change the heart.
But they can restrain the heartless"

Martin Luther King Jr.

Our Prime Minister Dr. Manmohan Singh is on record voicing the sentiment that the justice delivery system of our country needs to be humanized to a far greater degree than it is at present. He has been of the considered view that our justice system needs to be tailored more to the needs of the poorest of the people. Hearing this view, one's mind immediately relates back to October 1958 **when Nani Palkivala portrayed the great Chief Justice M.C. Chagla in the words: "To the Romans, justice was a Goddess whose symbols were – a throne of justice that tempests could not shake, a pulse that passion could not stir, eyes that were blind to any feeling of favour or ill will, and the sword that fell on all offenders with equal certainty and impartial strength. This Goddess brooded over the Chief Justices court. But her stern features relented into a compassionate smile and the language of the statute was sometimes subjected to serve strain when one of the parties before the court was of humble and lowly class."**

One hopes that the compassionate smile and humane attitude remains no longer limited to the legendary judges of the past, but permeates all courts without exception. For achieving this lofty vision, a process of sensitization to human suffering needs to be initiated at both the micro as well as the macro level. Introspection and soul searching by persons piloting the judicial machinery is the need of the hour. What is required today is deeply sensitive, proactive and innovative judges. In his latest book 'India's Legal System: can it be saved', Fali S. Nariman, the noted jurist, stresses the crying need for 'robust judging'. He feels that the trial judge is the eyes and ears of every case. Being not merely a recorder of facts, but a surveyor of all evidence, a good trial judge needs to have a 'third ear', that is to hear and comprehend even what has not been said. A material witness not recalling the major details must immediately invoke the suspicions of the 'truth-seeking Judge'. Nariman feels that for this, no new law is required. The requirement is only common sense and acquaintance with the facts of life. One cannot help, but totally agree with Nariman's point. However, for translating his vision into reality, the mindset clogged by precedents and tradition has to be modified to suit the present day needs of society. **One is constantly reminded of what John Dryden once remarked "Reasons to rule, but mercy to forgive: The first is law, the last prerogative".**

EVERY ONE HAS A RIGHT TO LIVE UNDER THE INDIAN CONSTITUTION

"Rather suffer an injustice than commit one"

Yiddish Proverb

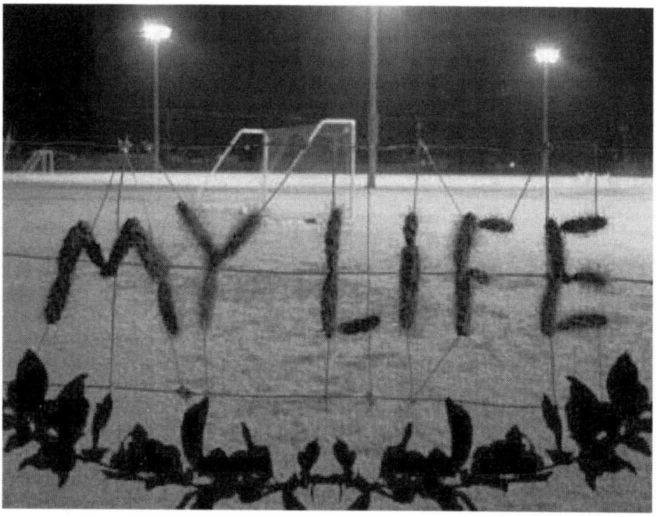

Memories are vivid when the television announced deaths due to starvation in Rajasthan's Baran district. One is surprised as to what is the level of accountability of the people who have been in power and one is so helpless seeing the blame game and the buck being passed from one to another. Does the Constitution not impose an obligation to uphold the right to life under Article 21? Earlier, such deaths were reported in Orissa in 2001 and in Madhya Pradesh's Shivpuri district. The governments have, as usual denied them and attributed these deaths to other causes like death due to sickness, old age, due to eating a traditional variety of grass or consuming mango Kernels.

It is a sad day for the nation to read about starvation deaths in India. There are more than 60 millions tones of cereals stacked in the warehouses of Food Corporation of India and various State Governments. Is this the kind of socialism that the founding father of our Constitution had contemplated? Is this the kind of social and economic justice the opening sentence to the Preamble of our Constitution promises? One wonders where is the right to life guaranteed by Article 21 of one of the worlds longest written Constitution has gone? The Supreme Court of India has been ruling time and again that right to life includes the right to food.

Let us presume for a moment that the deaths were actually not due to starvation but were caused by diseases or lack of medical care. Even in that case, is the health of the citizens not one of the primary duties of any responsible so called welfare state? The Supreme Court in the case of *Parmanand Katara* held that doctors assistance was a part of the citizens Right to Life under Article 21 of the Constitution. At times one also wonders as to whether the high sounding Constitutional concepts like **"Welfare State", "the Directive Principles of State governance", "the social and economic justice"** have any semblance with the ground realities of the daily life of an ordinary citizen? **Haven't these concepts become near bookish concepts when one hears of starvation deaths, suicides by farmers due to debts and selling or mortgaging of women and children?**

As a citizen one would like to know as to how many higher functionaries who were directly responsible for the maintenance of the public distribution system and for providing food for work have been hauled up and held accountable? The right to information under the new law of Information must be made more meaningful for the poor and neglected citizens of this Country.

THE MANNER OF DEATH PENALTY NEEDS TO BE MORE HUMANE

"Death, the one appointment we all must keep, and for which no time is set"

Charlie Chan

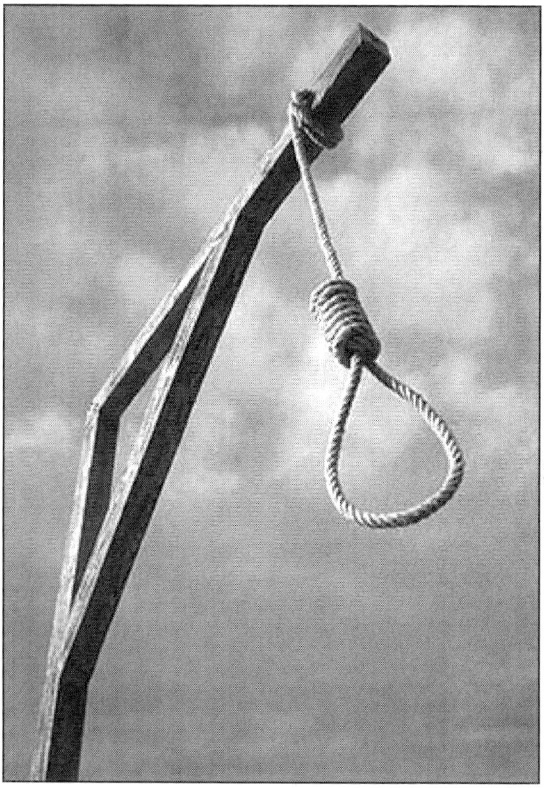

SECTION 354(5) Cr PC Mandates that when a convicted person is sentenced to death, he be hanged by the neck till he is dead.

In addition there are the old and technical prison manuals which laid down the mode of execution of a sentence of a person condemned to death. The prison manual requires that a manila rope, one inch in diameter shall be used for executions. The scale of drop of the body been proportioned to the weight of the culprit ranging from 5 feet to 7 feet, depending upon the discretion of the jail superintendent. It has further been laid down that the hands of the convict would be pinioned behind his back; his legs would be strapped tightly and his head covered with a cap and his body to remain suspended for half an hour. **Seeing this brutal manner of executing death in a civilized society one is reminded of the pain and remorse of Alfred Jodl when he remarked "Death - by hanging! - that, at least, I did not deserve. The death part - all right, somebody has to stand for the responsibility. But that - that I did not deserve!"**

Is it not important that even a person convicted of a heinous crime should be given a dignified manner of death and dignified burial? Is the hanging of a person in today's modern time not barbaric and an obsolete method of execution? In the United Kingdom from where we have borrowed most of our judicial precepts, the mode of execution by hanging has been done away with since it was found to be obsolete and barbaric.

The Law Commission of India has recommended switching over the mode of executing the death penalty from hanging to injecting the convict with intravenous doses of lethal injections. The whole process takes five to nine minutes consisting of a course of three pricks – the first one being a sedative. This is far more human in comparison to hanging because if the drop is not proper, a person might not break his spinal cord and could resultantly suffer the last agony for even up to 30 minutes.

The United Nations Economics and Social Council by a resolution in 1984 had appealed that death penalty should be carried out in a manner which caused least suffering to the convict.

Even in China, where executions by firing squads are routine matters there were as many as eight executions carried out in the year 2000 by means of the lethal injection. In the year 2001 over sixty death penalties were carried out through the lethal injections in the United States.

For an execution to be termed acceptable to society, it should be instantaneous and least painful. There should be least disfigurement and mutilation of the body because dignity even of the dead is a hallmark of any civilized society. **Ours is a reformative legal system and we need to reform the method of deaths by the due process of law. Only then can one agree with what Shakespeare remarked in Julius Caesar (Act 2, Sc 2)**

"Of all the wonders that I have yet heard,
It seems to me most strange that men should fear;
Seeing that death, a necessary end,
Will come when it will come."

THE POLICE IS BASICALLY FOR OUR PROTECTION

"The means for which we live;
have outdistanced the ends for which we live;
Our scientific power has outrun our spiritual power.
We have guided missiles,
and misguided men".

Martin Luther in 'Strength to Love'

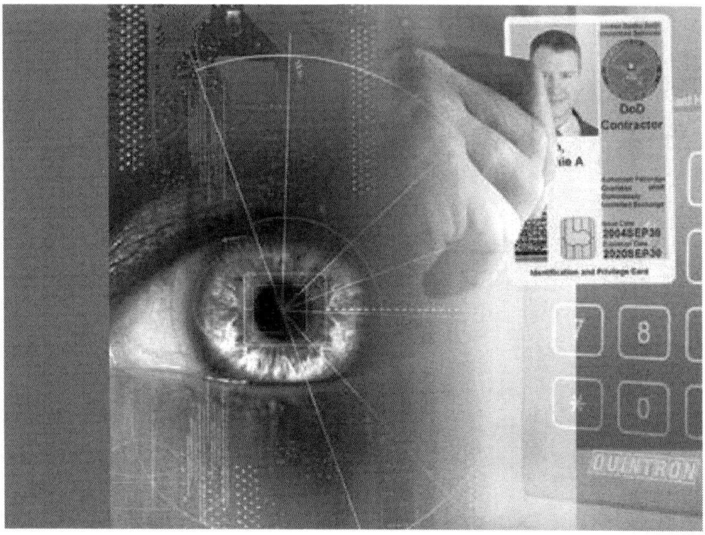

Reading the newspapers daily is depressing especially when one reads of so many crimes being committed by people in the Uniform. **Recent story of unarmed helpless citizens demanding clean drinking water in Bombay being mercilessly beaten and one of them losing his life for water is a slur on the Indian Policing System.** Though this is true of many security forces but the instances of the police excesses and unbecoming actions are multiplying with each passing day. The

Despatch of the Court of Directors dated September 24, 1856 lamented, "The police in India has lamentably failed in accomplishing the ends for which it was established is a notorious fact. That it is all but useless for the prevention and sadly inefficient for the detection of crime is generally admitted. Unable to check crime, it is with rare exceptions, unscrupulous as to its mode of wielding the authority with which it is armed for the functions it fails to fulfil and has a very general character for corruption and oppression."

Many police officials, from DGPs to the head constables, are facing action for crimes ranging from torture to murder to molestation.

We regularly witness many glaring examples of police atrocities, despite the fact that the Supreme Court in *D.K. Basu's* case has chalked out various do's and don'ts by the police during arrest and detention and has made police officials liable for contempt in cases of default. **It is time that courts forge new tools to effectively implement the social protection judgments. One such measure could be the appointment of standing judicial commissioners to oversee the implementation of various judgments. This would definitely be a departure from the conventional judicial orthodoxy, but aggressive non-conventional approaches have to be adopted in emergent situations in order to rise to the occasion. In fact, our law does permit the appointment of local commissioners. Thus, this concept will have to be extended with certain innovations and variations to meet the situation.**

In early 70's, the Supreme Court in *Rudul Sah's* case has come out with an novel approach and has now started awarding interim compensation for State excesses, but for making the necessary impact the quantum and frequency of compensation need to be increased.

There is also a need to strictly implement the existing provisions of law in curtailing the wide powers of the police. Section 54 of the CrPC deals with the right to medical examination, whereas Section 176 of the Act postulates a magisterial enquiry into the cause of death of a person in police custody.

The Parliament of the Country could enact a Fundamental Right which would ensure accountability of the policemen. **In cases of police excesses, a rebuttable presumption operating against the defaulting policemen could also be legislated.**

"Silence Nourishes Oppression".

President Mitterrand

THE FOUNDATIONS OF LAW NEED TO BE STRENGTHENED WITH TRUTH

"All Sides in a trial want to hide
At least some of the truth".

Alan Dershowitz
Lawyer and Harvard Law Professor

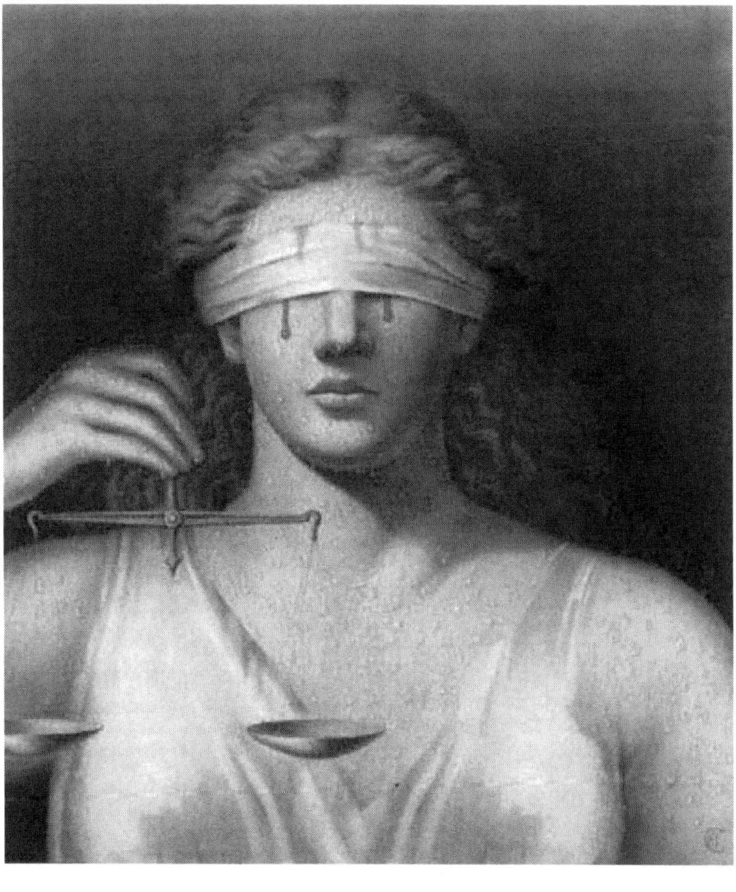

The National sentiment has been that truth would ultimately be victorious over all tests and tribulations. This is a declaration that the Indian Nation is well proud of.

The Malimath Committee which recently recommended reform of criminal justice, it also made an all out effort at re-establishing truth in court working. The importance of doing this cannot be overstated. The business of the court is to administer justice – what justice can there be without truth? The measures suggested are far reaching and framed so as to ensure that falsehood does not have too long an innings in court functioning.

Malimath seeks that the Preamble to the Code of Criminal Procedure amended to read: "Quest for truth shall be the foundation of the criminal justice system ... It shall be the duty of every functionary of the criminal justice system and everyone associated with it in the administration of justice to actively pursue the quest for truth."

It has thus been suggested to make adequate provisions along with Section 311 CrPC. Below this section it has been suggested that a provision be made along the following lines:

"Any court shall at any stage of inquiry or trial under this code, have such power to issue directions to the investigating officers to make further investigation or to direct the supervisory officer to take appropriate action for proper or adequate investigation so as to assist the court in the search for truth".

Section 482 of the Code is sought to be amended to arm the courts with powers to make appropriate orders necessary to discover truth.

These are very beneficial recommendations that will enlarge the court's inherent powers and better equip it to uncover the truth. These recommendations, if implemented would go a long way in removing the procedural and jurisdictional constraints of courts.

It has also been observed that routinely, witnesses give false evidence. In a majority of the cases these tutored witnesses escape liability for lying under oath since the legal procedure for taking action against perjury is cumbersome and impracticable. **Malimath has done well by advising amendment to Section 344 Cr PC to enable the court to try summarily for giving wilful false evidence.** It has been recommended to enhance the sentence from three months to two years imprisonment.

Our salvation lies in adopting and following letter and spirit the recommendations of this great committee so that the malice of a high acquittal rate of more than 90% in criminal proceedings can also be corrected.

HANDLE OUR LESS FORTUNATE HANDICAPPED BRETHREN WITH CARE

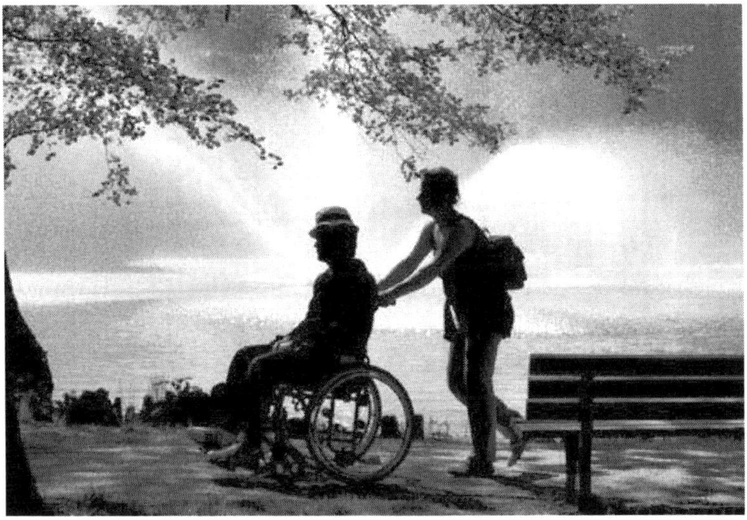

Of late a statistic survey has been done about the less fortunate segment of Indian society *i.e.* the handicapped. Going by one such survey as per about 1.9 per cent. of India's total population have physical or sensory disabilities which includes visual, speech, hearing and loco-motor disabilities. Although India has legislated upon the 1995 Disability Act, this is not enough. **The US Supreme Court (*Olmstead* versus *LC*) has ruled that states must provide community placements for individuals with disabilities.** India must take cue from international developments. Krystina Mrugalska, of America's Disability Rights Movement, gave vent to his feelings by expressing on the Day of Dignity in the terms that, "let us not delude ourselves into thinking that disability only concerns the disabled person. It is a problem of the entire society.

India enacted the Disabilities Act, 1995 as an aftermath to the Beijing meeting of December 1992 and the proclamation of the Economic and Social Commission for Asian and Pacific Region. India, being a signatory to the proclamation, a special onus is cast on us to give effect to the laudable objects of the proclamation.

The Disability Act, 1995 has been invented with the basic purpose of rehabilitation of persons with disabilities. Rehabilitation involves the process by which persons with disabilities could reach and maintain optimal physical, sensory intellectual, psychiatric and social functional levels.

India has been a trendsetter in enacting a special enactment known as "The National Trust for Welfare of Persons with Autism, Cerebral Palsy, Mental Retardation and Multiple Disabilities Act, 1999". The main goal of this legislation is to provide infrastructure and funds management for the purpose of charting out affirmative actions in favour of persons covered under the Act. A National Trust has also been provided for under this Act.

But despite India's commitment, the handicapped still have to fight for basic rights. Javed Abidis' recent fast unto death espouses the cause of 45 million disabled voters for a barrier free access to polling booths. Activists from Deafway, National Blind Association and Leprosy Mission have joined Abidi in his crusade for their rights. A barrier free entry to the various polling booths need to be allowed to the less fortunate population during the elections. **In America the Supreme Court in the case of *Olmstead* versus *LC* has held that the states must provide community placements for individuals with disabilities.** We in India would do better if we were to focus more on the implementation of the recent enactments of mid and late nineties.

INDIA NEEDS ITS OWN MODEL OF THE JURY SYSTEM

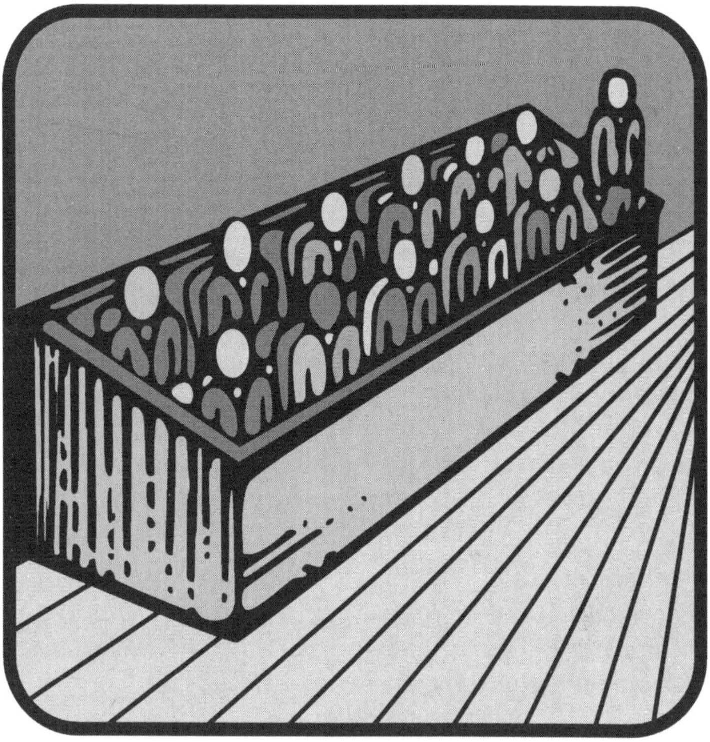

The Supreme Court of India had taken a well considered decision in ordering a retrial of the Best Bakery case in Maharashtra as Gujarat was not found conducive to a fair trial.

It is time for national rethinking on the lines as to how to ensure fair trials and rule out any possibilities of collusions between the accused and the prosecution. It is time one thought of giving a try to the jury system in instances of heinous crimes and of genocide.

The English jury generally date back to around the *Magna Carta* in 1215. In trial by jury the judgment being by ones' peers', it was intended to act as a restraint on Royal Action. The cut off date of 1215 as the beginning of the jury system is important since earlier to this guilt or innocence was decided in various ways, the most common being trial by battle or by a similar method.

In England and the Wales, the jury alone would decide innocence or guilt by deliberating in secret and forming a collective view on facts to form a verdict. As far as the verdict is concerned, after the jury retires, none may interfere, and historically, as illustrated by Pope, juries were locked in a room to deliberate their verdict without food or drink. **The facts of a case were always the province of the jury and the judges role was limited to decide the law. The judge would give the jury appropriate directions on the law and sum up the facts to the jury.** English juries played no part in the sentencing process.

In some situations the role of jury trial exceeded beyond the juries role of being 'fair fact finders' at criminal trials. This has been depicted by K. Dubrovskys' observations regarding the jury in BUSHELL'S case in 1670 whereby he remarked that jury's role was instrumental in establishing freedom of religion, the right to free assembly and freedom of speech.

We in India could also try to experiment with limiting the role of jury to 'fair fact finding' in criminal matters of vital importance. To make the system more effective, the jury could be selected from a panel of local people of high stature. The experiment of the jury system in India keeping the various social and economic factors in view while developing the model tailor made to Indian conditions would be a good idea in which we all have nothing to loose.

PUBLIC INTEREST BEING PROTECTED THROUGH LAW COURTS

"Justice, though she's painted blind is to the weaker side inclined".

Samuel Butler (17th Century English satirical poet)

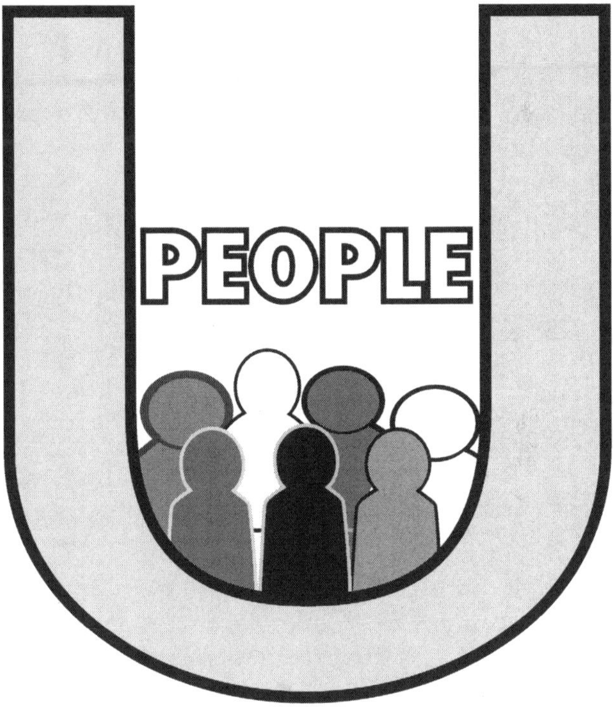

PUBLIC INTEREST is a new kind of litigation brought about by the Constitutional Courts like the High Courts and the Supreme Court of India. These kinds of cases were given birth to by way of a simple telegram to the Supreme Court by a member of the public in the last few decades. Prior to this there have been provisions in the CPC dealing with public interest. For example, Section 91 dealt with public nuisance and Order 1, Rule 8 of the Code of Civil Procedure permitted one to act on behalf of all in the same interest. Though these provisions had been there in law for many years but their social impact was negligible. But what really is the present day PIL as we all understand it?

As per the report of the Council for Public Interest Law set up by Ford foundation of the USA (1976 at pp. 6-7) PIL was defined as : "Public interest law is the name that has recently been given to efforts to provide legal representation to groups and interests, which were not represented previously. Such efforts have been undertaken in recognition that ordinary market place for legal services fail to provide services to significant segments of the population and to significant interests. Such groups and interests include the poor, the environmentalists, the consumer, the racial and ethnic minorities".

The Supreme Court adopted an original approach and it was for the first time in free India that telegrams and post cards were treated as petitions.

By the mid-eighties, the Indian Courts had adopted a very activist approach and have started interfering in almost anything and everything. The thin lines demarcating the executive and judicial boundaries have become even thinner. Probably, this judicial intervention was required for the times we are in, since the executive had virtually become ineffective. **The courts took on to themselves the functions of directing operation cleanups, of cleansing of the environment; of applying the balm on inmates of jails, etc.**

It was finally a judge who had to unlock the chains of the prisoners fetters in *Prem Shanker Shukla's* case;

it was also a judge who had to stop torture in *Sunil Batra's* and *Sheela Barse's* cases. It was further a judge only who had to issue the warning against police excesses in *D.K. Basu's* case. It was only because of the effect of PILs that today we can walk with freedom and breathe cleaner air in Delhi. Thanks to the *M.C. Mehta's* case which finally replaced the diesel engines with the CNGs.

People now feared that with such widespread judicial interference, the flood gates of litigation would be opened wide and the already over burdened courts would get further slowed down. To this seen the Apex Court of India itself answered in Prof. K.E. Scotts' words that the "Idle and whimsical plaintiff, a dilettante who litigates for a lark, is a spectre which haunts legal literature, not the court room".

The courts have a extremely challenging task ahead of them especially when systems in the country are on the verge of breaking down.

'Laws and Institutions require to be adapted, not to good men, but to bad.'

John Stuart Mill (1806-73)

LAW NEEDS TO BE CHANGED TO CONTROL EPIDEMIC OF ACCIDENTS ON INDIAN ROADS

"Nothing is more subject to change than the Laws"

Michael De Montaigne
(16th Century French writer)

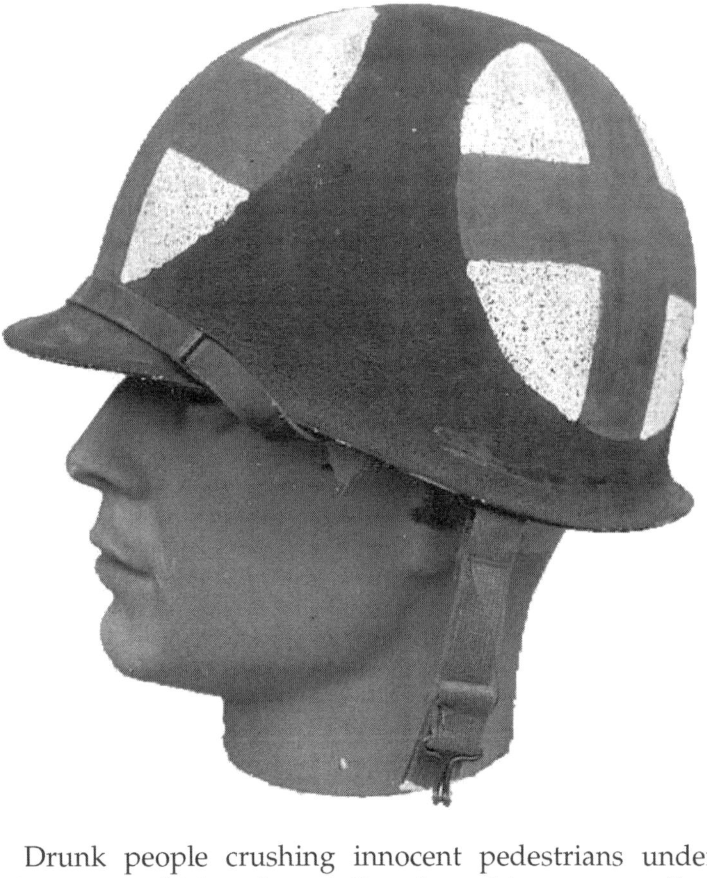

Drunk people crushing innocent pedestrians under their motor vehicles, the privileged crushing poor cyclists on the streets of Metropolitan towns is becoming a daily scene. The thoughtless bus drivers are callously cutting tickets to the grave of innocent persons. Helpless commuters being crushed to death by killer vehicles has become a commonplace scene on the Indian roads! This phenomenon has assumed dangerous proportions.

According to researches at the World Bank and automobile associations, India has one of the world's largest auto-related fatalities. Each year approximately 60,000 people are killed in vehicle accidents, besides heavy disabilities. In a given year more than 3,00,000 accidents are reported. Studies on accidents the world over, have shown that the human factor is responsible for a majority of the accidents. In India, vehicle users are the causative factor in 70 per cent. of the road accidents.

This dangerous scene is made all the more tragic by the presence of a weak law and a indifferent police. Hence, there is a general feeling of complacency, "I can manage attitude", as generally the culprit is allowed to get off the hook by mere light charges under Sections 279 and 304A of the IPC. **The law on the point is highly inadequate since Section 304A of the IPC only provides a maximum sentence of two years imprisonment.**

One wonders why the police do not book the accidental death cases for culpable homicide under Section 304 of the IPC, as this would provide some deterrence. Finally, a stricter law is required. **In the case of *Jennings* v. *US Government*, (1983) IAC 624, it was ruled that in cases of accidental, deaths, the drivers of the vehicle could be charged with manslaughter.**

Of course, though it is true that a stricter law on the issue will give far more powers to the police and a few innocents may also come under the law, but this will help in creating a kind of fear psychosis among people, and drivers will begin to behave properly on roads. However, safeguards can be provided for honest implementation of the new law.

The system of issuing driving licenses needs to be streamlined and overhauled. Each time, does the police have to wait till a person is actually hit? Why don't the law enforcers and law makers take preemptive measures so that many lives can be saved?

CURBING THE MENACE OF ROAD ACCIDENTS

"One death is a tragedy
one million a statistic"

Joseph Stalin (Soviet Dictator)

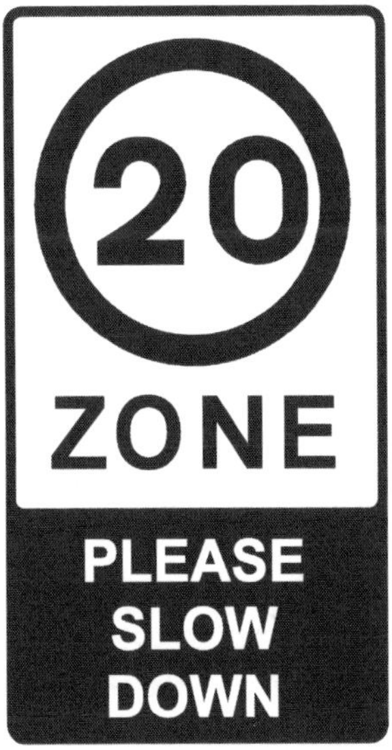

The police all over are booking drivers for rash and negligent driving. This malice has assumed the proportions of an epidemic and drunken driving is also species of this problem. Its a free-for-all situation on the Indian roads and human life has been greatly discounted as is evident from mere look on the Indian road. **A World Bank study says that in terms of auto-related fatalities, India is among the world's worst.** Nationwide, more than 56,000 people die in road accidents each year. America's road accident fatalities number only about 35,000 despite the fact that USA has far more vehicle than India.

Accidents caused by mechanical failure are very few in number. **The major cause lies in human error.** Over speeding, rash and drunken driving, and overtaking, especially from the left, are some of the gray areas that need immediate attention of our Traffic police. Strict implementation of the Motor Vehicles Act and the Indian Penal Code are of paramount importance. Without proper implementation of the law there can be no public order and this is particularly true of our roads.

Section 184 of the Motor Vehicles Act, 1988, which provides upto six months imprisonment term for dangerous driving, needs rigorous implementation. This provision prohibits driving a vehicle at a speed or in a manner dangerous to the public.

Section 185 of the Act bans driving while under intoxication – defined as a blood-alcohol level exceeding 30 mg per 100 ml blood. It also applies to driving under the influence of drugs. It is time that the police administration became more focused in their attempt to check drunken and rash driving. Section 203 specially provides for breath tests for checking the alcohol level in the blood. Consistent use of breathalyzers by the Traffic police is long over due. Even the Indian Penal Code under Section 279 makes rash driving a cognizable offence punishable with six months imprisonment whereas Section 336 IPC makes any rash or negligent act endangering human life penal with a three months term.

One serious lacuna pertains to non-motorised vehicles. Errors by drivers of animal driven transport and by cyclists can also result in fatalities but one never sees Traffic police challaning these offenders. Likewise, vehicles carrying excess or awkward loads are a hazard on the roads, yet they ply unchecked.

We in India have made great leaps in human technology. **Now it is time that we aim at introducing**

computerized navigation systems in motor vehicles. This will eliminate human error to a great extent. In the USA, such devices are already coming into the market, For example, many new car models have cruise control – a device that sets the speed of the vehicle. Other devices integrate computers with 360 radar-scanners that warn of potentially hazardous situations. It will take some time before these devices are available in India. Now it is largely dependent upon the Traffic police to gear up to face the grim road accident situation and implement the existing law in letter and sprit.

JUSTICE IN INDIA IS VERY BELATED

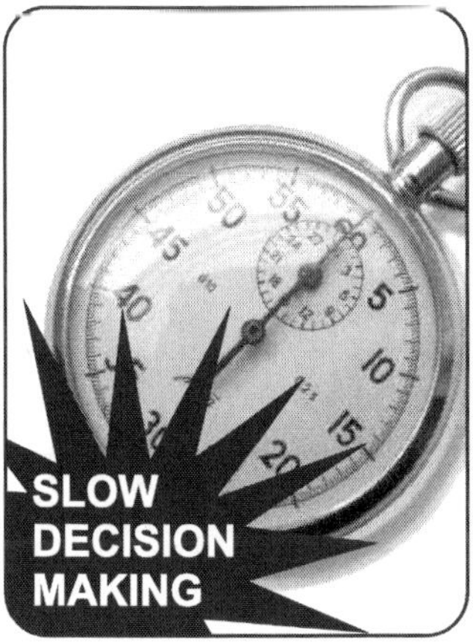

"Though Justice moves slowly, it seldom fails to overtake the wicked".

Horace
(1st Century B.C. Roman Poet)

It has been a common experience that justice in India in many important cases is delivered after such great delay that its effect is totally diluted. Cases of such type as those of the Delhi Riots, Uphar Cinema Fire tragedy, and many other instances which go unnoticed. With this result, what happens in practice is that many of the key accused get acquitted and very valuable evidence is lost. The major accused gets declared innocent since their guilt could not be proved beyond reasonable doubt.

Indeed, many an accused are being let off on procedural issues. Having waited for over 18 years in the case of Delhi riots, many of the widows have already died without seeing the culprits behind bars. The recent example of the Liberahan Commission submitting its report on an issue having national ramnifications after 17 years which should have ordinarily taken maximum six months speaks volumes.

The cries of the victims of the Uphaar Cinema and Bhopal tragedies are still haunting the corridors of justice.

Where has Article 21's guarantee of speedy justice gone? The slow paced judicial system has become a matter of serious national concern.

We are today seeing justice in slow motion. The tragedy of the system is that the slow process itself punishes all those who come in contact with it – the winner as well as the loser.

A system which allows heinous culprits to escape the clutches of law needs serious review and overhaul. One wonders why even in the most heinous crimes the courts insist on the prosecution to prove the case beyond a reasonable doubt and the slightest of doubt regarding the accused's complicity in the crime results in his acquittal.

One wonders why the law is not made simpler and more understandable. The judgment should be delivered on the principle of greater probability. Could a concept of the civil law be not incorporated to the criminal law, wherein a judge will be able to decide in favour of the most probable version warranted by the facts.

Justice should be put on fast tracks to be speeded up since there are 23.4 million pending cases in various High Courts and subordinate courts.

In fact, rigid time limit for disposal of the case needs to be prescribed in various categories. **In the United States of America a 180-day deadline has been prescribed for disposing of a criminal matter, whereas in Japan there is a system of discretionary prosecution in the administration of criminal justice.**

The Japanese Code of Criminal Procedure provides for the Public Prosecutor to disapprove to prosecute any case if he considers it unnecessary in the light of gravity of offences and various other conditions. The Indian System can learn from the plus points of various successful systems all over the world.

CONSTITUTIONAL COURTS CAN BE TREND SETTERS FOR SPEEDING UP JUSTICE

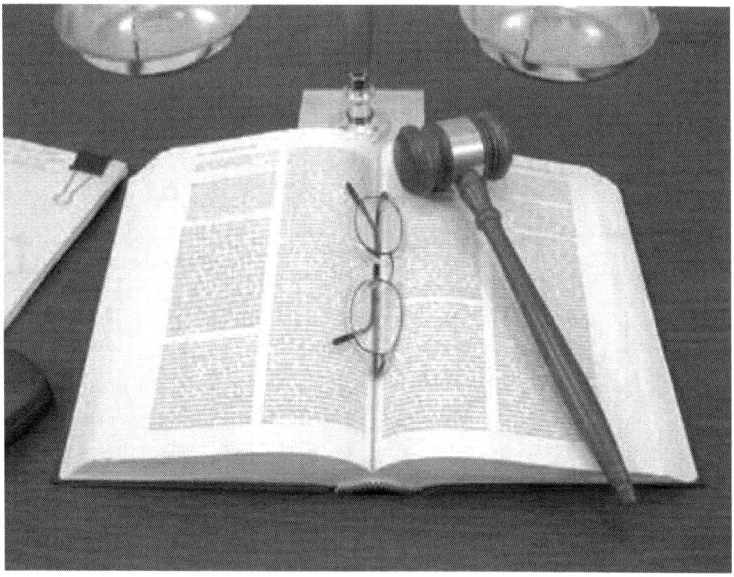

"Docket crises" has been a long standing problem faced by various courts all over the country. The various High Courts in the country have an arrears figure as high as 30.4 million pending cases. According to the Report of Crime in India, 2000 published by the National Crime Bureau, 49,21,710 criminal cases under the IPC were pending at the end of the year 2000.

The country's experiment with the fast track courts has yet to create the necessary impact. The concept of this species of courts has not been able to deliver in many of the states. There is a dire need for rigorous implementation of the fast track scheme. There are infrastructural limitations and the problem of finding suitable persons to man these courts.

The Malimath Committee has suggested the setting up of an Arrears Eradication Scheme on similar lines of the fast track courts project. The scheme is scripted to eradicate the arrears pending within a record time of five years. It suggests the functioning of courts on part time basis with part time judges by adjustments with regular courts.

For effective crises management concerted and focused action is required. **It is the regular courts, which will have to be geared up rather than finding a via media of complementing the regular courts with part time ones**.

But Malimath Committee's suggestions to increase the number of offences that could be compounded could prove effective. Extending this benefit to pending cases could result in the disposal by settlement of many an old cases. It will also be meaningful that all summons cases be tried under Section 262 of the Criminal Procedure Code. Thus, the process of justice could be speeded up on various counts and the slow judicial process can be put into fast motion by the measures listed above.

RESCHEDULING INDIAN JUSTICE AT THE GRASS-ROOT LEVEL

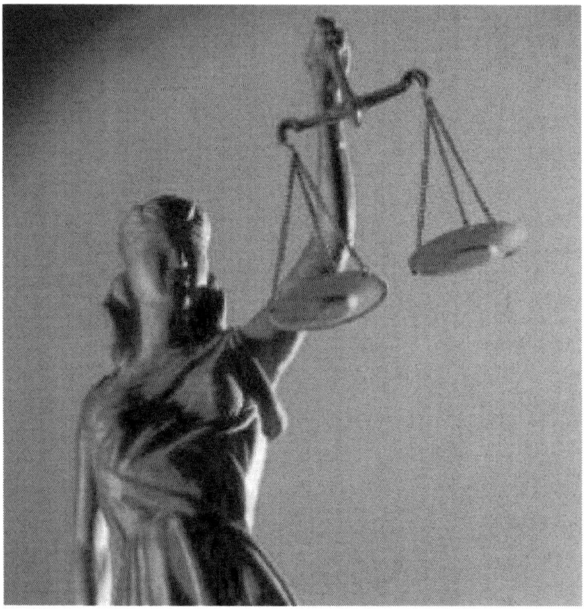

The Central Government has proposed 1.5 lakh 'Nyaya Panchayats' which can be a major initiative at rescheduling the Indian justice schedule. Its step in the right direction in arriving at the basic issues at the grass-root label.

Resolving local civil disputes and petty crimes are high on the Government's agenda. The Gram Nayayalaya Act of Madhya Pradesh is a pioneer in this direction. To this, the Chief Justice of India's resolve to put the cases of persons holding public positions on fast track can be a great impetus to quick delivery of justice. The experiment of changing the track of justice to the fast lane has proved beneficial in many states with lakhs of cases being disposed off under the 'F....T....S'.

It is hard to believe, but operating within the same Indian conditions, a Jodhpur-based fast track court had handed over a life-term to rapists of a German tourist in just 20 days. The crime was committed on May 11, 2005, the challan filed on the May 16 and the additional sessions judge sentenced two rapists to life imprisonment on June 1. There is now a hope for revival of the system and resolving of the 'docket-crises'. To add on to this momentum, the implementation of certain crisis management measures is important.

The alternate disputes redressal system does need to be further strengthened so that there can be a decongestion of cases, both at the pre-trial and trial stages.

India has recently incorporated the American module of plea-bargaining by bringing in Section 265(A-L) in the Code of Criminal Procedure. This practice needs to be encouraged by courts for attaining zero pendency. In the Criminal Code, there is also a provision under Section 13 for the appointment of special judicial magistrates by the High Court for tenure of upto one year. This provision could also come handy in grappling with the huge pendency. Reportedly, an HCS officer Abhe Singh in his Ph.D research paper advocated the appointment of legal assistants to every judge individually for specialized and expert handling of the heavy cause list. Further, the ongoing computerization would help. Standardisation of the settled case law instead of citing individual authorities on every issue also needs attention.

Listing only of completed cases before the various Benches would save judicial time. This has already been done in certain High Courts. As propriate delegation, wherever possible and permissible, would be a people-friendly measure. Curtailing the length of pleadings and of judgments is long overdue. **Justice M.C. Chagla, in his autobiography 'Roses in December', advocates**

short judgments supported with the latest authority of the highest court. This holds true even today. Asher Rubin, the then California Deputy Attorney General, on a request for filing a brief exceeding the court's 50-page limit remarked: "The issues can be analysed in pages less than fifty, if plaintiffs could with thoughts and words endeavour to be thrifty."

But let us not forget that the punch line is to increase the ratio of the judge and the population. We are far behind the ratio of many an advanced nations.

CLIMBING THE MOUNTAIN OF PENDING CASES

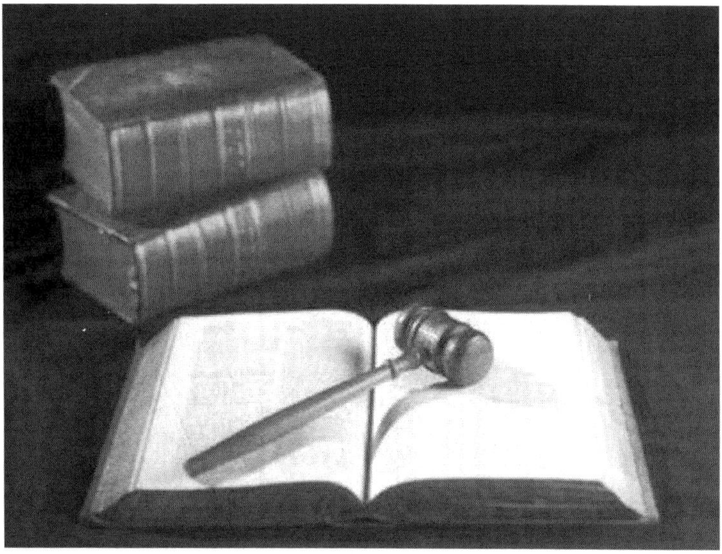

The legal luminaries have been giving wake up calls to the legal fraternity from time to time to deal with the stupendous task of the mounting arrears which has resulted in huge pendency. It is high time that we tackle the docket crises which has a magnitude of more than three crore cases pending adjudication in our country.

Many an eminent persons have voised various solutions for tackling the elephantine problem of piled up court cases. They are all unanimous that this problem must be given the highest national priority for upholding the rule of law. A few have suggested that the alternate dispute redressal measures. This alternate dispute redressal mechanism warrants a national initiative. It is high time we act on the jurists advice, least we have to regret in the words of **Andre Gide**, the French thinker, who once remarked, **"Everything has been said already, but as no one listens, we must always begin again."**

The pendency problem is a direct consequence of justice in slow motion. Unfortunately, it is felt that the slow justice delivery system punishes all those who come in contact with it – the winner as well as the loser.

Seeing the speed with which some fast track courts are delivering verdicts within only a few days proves the point that constraints of systems are no limiting factors for certain individuals in dispensing instant justice. However, updating the justice delivery system is long overdue. Mere cosmetic changes will no longer serve the purpose.

India is definitely making efforts to tune in to the world over developments with the launch of the Rs. 854 crore plan by the Prime Minister to transform the Indian courts into paper-less courts. By such measures India will emulate the US and Singapore examples by launching the new internet technology court rooms of the 21st century. We need to give a further impetus to establishing e-courts, pressing the internet into service, and achieving greatest speed and accuracy in the justice delivery system. It is high time that we also digitalize the voluminous court records.

WE NEED MORE JUDGES

Our Attorney General had once voiced his judicial priorities. He had made it clear that speeding up of the judicial process was high up on the judicial agenda. The concern for the slow pace of justice is justified in view of National Crime Record Bureau statistics putting the criminal cases pendency in the year 2000 at 49,21,710. It has been remarked in the epoch making case of *Jennison* v. *Baker*, (1972) 1 All ER 997 that "Law should not sit limply, while those who defy it go free and those who seek its protection lose hope." Even during the late nineteenth eighties the Law Commission of India, in its 120th report, favoured raising the number of Judges in India from 10.5 to 50 per million as in USA. The number was 107; at that time the Judge-population ratio per million was 41.6 in Australia, 50.9 in England and 75.2 in Canada. This fact was also judicially observed by the Supreme Court's seven-judge Bench in the case of *P. Rama Chandra Rao* v. *State of Karnataka*, JT 2002 (4) SC 92.

In todays' situation the Indian judge is highly over worked with the weight of dockets compared to his counter-parts in other areas of operation. It is thus important to give him space by increasing the numerical strength of judges and the bringing down the judge-population ratio. Law is the very creative field and even judges need space. Regarding this issue of workload, the Supreme Court has described it in *All India Judges Association* case (AIR 1993 SC 2493 Para 25) thus "The sedentary work is mainly of two types –mechanical and creative. Each case coming before the judge has its own peculiarities requiring application of fresh mind and skill. The judge has constantly to be a creative artist. His work, therefore, requires constant thinking and display of talent. The exertions involved in the duties of the judge cannot be compared with the duties of other services."

India has a serious docket crises and there is a clear 23.4 million cases backlog going by the last available statistics. The road to justice is some time so long that it takes decades for a case to be decided. Ultimately even if it is decided in once favour, the long wait has already taken the steam out of even the winner. In such situations remedying the delay is of paramount importance. It is thus imperative to increase the judge population ratio and bring it in conformity with the ratio of the legal systems the world over because **finally justice needs judges.**

THE INDIAN I.T. ACT IS A LEGISLATION IN THE RIGHT DIRECTION

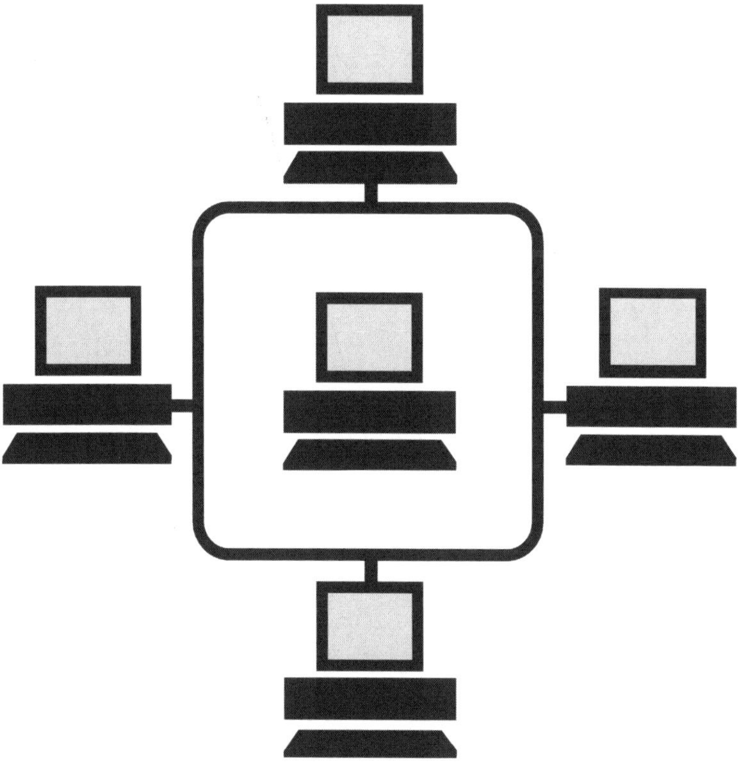

Updating the working of the Indian Judicial System is long over due. The working needs to be streamlined and greater order in the functioning is required. The buildings are old and are ill-equipped to handle such a heavy overload of cases. That is why there is hardly any space in the outdated Court premises to even accommodate the decades old records of various cases. The libraries are ill-equipped and all is not well with the court administration. **India is in the book of records not for any major achievements in any vital field but we are in record books because we have to our credit or rather discredit the longest litigation or some citizens supports the longest nails or moustache.** The Limca book of record quotes the case of Hunumantha Reddi whose battle against his supersession lasted with the government for 44 years 9 months and 8 days in the court of law.

In this background the passing of the Information Technology Act, 2000 has come as a breath of fresh air. Now electronic governance, secure electronic records and digital signatures have been recognized. Earlier, in 1990 the National Informatics Centre (NIC) had started the much required project for computerization of the Supreme Court and the various High Courts in the country. This enabled the list of business to be displayed on the various computers and Internet. It also helped in automating and scheduling of cases to be heard by various courts. The judgment information system was introduced. Infact, the State of Andhra Pradesh has proved to be a forerunner by providing for the production of an under trial before a magistrate through video linkage to enable a speedy and transparent trial. This will also result in substantial reduction of expense and resources since as about 1000 constable were engaged in escorting prisoners to courts daily.

With these innovations, the Supreme Court and High Courts now being just a click of the mouse away from the common man an all out efforts needs to be made for using the innovative technology for the good of the common man. The Supreme Court of India has started the filing of cases through e-mail and this should be followed by the various High Courts and the Subordinate Courts of the entire country. The affidavits could also be sent through the new E-filing system since digital signatures have now been recognized by the latest IT Act. The technology can also be used for creating an information data bank on personnel, and other aspects of courts administration. Fiscal and report management, simultaneous translation of various judgments and court proceedings can be other areas in which the latest technology can be used more extensively in order to make justice more people friendly. Only then will it be able to grapple with the Herculean task of clearing 30.4 million pending cases in the country. Recently judge Valerie Pearlman at Southwark Crown Court South London who was hospitalized because of a major illness finished a criminal trial over the Internet right from her hospital bed. Her path breaking achievement was enabled by directing the jury from a great distance of many miles through the medium of a video link.

LET US MAKE JUSTICE MODERN AND UPDATED

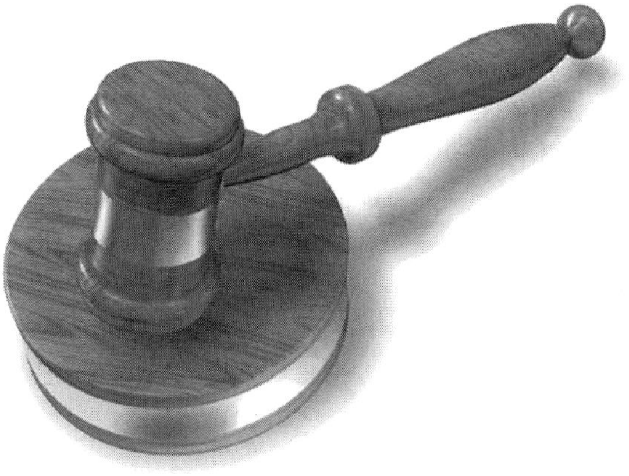

There have been acquittals in many cases after decades of protracted trials. A point in the case is an example of the Bofors where the acquittal was pronounced after more than 15 years. This results in lose – lose situation where not only the loser, but also the winner suffers The case pendency situation in our country is precarious with various High Courts having about 30.4 million pending cases.

As per the reporter of Crimes in India 2000 published by the National Crime Bureau, 49,21,710 criminal cases under the IPC were pending at the end of the year 2000. We must adjust to the latest technological developments the world over for a quick justice delivery system. The traditional thought process of our judges will have to the transformed into a computer friendly mindset through proper orientation and training. **Recently, Judge Valeria Pearlman in South England conducted a trial over the**

internet by guiding the jury over long distance from her hospital bed due to an acute illness. India has done well by recently enacting the Information and Technology Act, 2000, which has accorded legitimacy to the digital signatures and electronic records. Recently, the United States William and Mary Law School has set up Courtroom 21 – the new internet technology courtroom of the 21st century for trial and appellate work. Singapore has not lagged behind and has successfully innovated the Technology Court with a local area network (LAN) with an internet connection and is using latest concept of imaging, multimedia and video conferencing.

The E-courts in India, when they become a living reality, would enable the filing of complaints to courts through the e-mail and payment of court-fees through credit cards. Public case filing computerized centres could be set up by the government at various district headquarters in India for access to the general public at large. They could be on the lines of E-Sampark centres networked all over the country. Recently, the Supreme Court has embarked upon the innovative and ambitious plan of enabling the litigant to file cases through the system of e-filing. If this precedent is extended to the courts all over the country it was result in saving great time and money for the common men and would be one of the most people friendly measure.

USING TECHNOLOGY FOR NATIONAL SERVICE

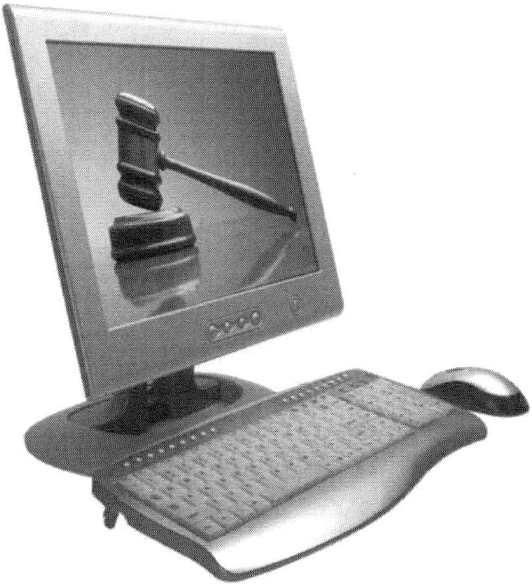

A soothsayer had predicted that a time would come when shopping would be done on computers. After some time, the arrival of internet and credit cards has made the prophecy come out true. Developments across the globe are also leading towards an electronic revolution with people contemplating a future in which the judge could be replaced by the computer. Roger Penrose, the Oxfordian had concluded his thesis with the premise that the computer will only compliment the judge and justice will always require judges. But the e-revolution will make the justice delivery machinery much more prompt and efficient. The New Information Technology Act of the year 2000 has granted the seal of approval to e-governance, digital records and electronic signatures. Former President Abdul Kalam had talked about implementing the concept of mobile courts. The Former Law Minister of State for Justice P.C.Thomas had declared the release Rs. 1200 crore for the computerization of 600 district courts across the country. Certain Jurists have expounded their vision of linking district courts being through video conferencing. This change in the mindset of the men who matter can catapult the nation into phenomenal progress. The experiment of video conferencing in Andhra Pradesh has proved very beneficial. Earlier, under trials were being escorted from jail to the courts by deploying about 1000 police constables daily. This technological innovation of video conferencing has resulted in saving substantial time and manpower. Video conferencing based evidence gathering has recently been started in the Karnatka High Court.

As per the Australian Law Reforms Commission, technology could be used in pre-trial and trial processes and in case-management. In U.K., the Lord Wolf Commission has stated that computers and telecommunications will play a significant role in supporting the proposed judicial reforms. In India, if the huge back log of pending cases in various High Courts itself has to be tackled, there is a pressing need for introducing the e-filing system on the pattern of many developed nations. The EFS should provide service in core areas such as electronic filing; electronic extract service, documentation and information service. Information kiosks in court premises could be beneficial. The pending cases information could be given through the Interactive Voice Response (IVR) system.

The concept of computerized courtrooms has been successfully implemented by the United States in Court Room Number 21 (New Technology Courtroom of the 21st Century) that is located at the College of William and Mary Law School. The Singapore Supreme Court has also set up a Technology Court which has a Local Area Network (LAN) with an internet connection and provides the use of multimedia, imaging and video conferencing. In the next decade India too, should have its own "Courtroom Number 21" in each district and State head quarters. Technology will thus be able to serve a great social purpose for our citizens.

UPHAAR CINEMA VERDICT: A BREAKTHROUGH IN COMPENSATION LAW

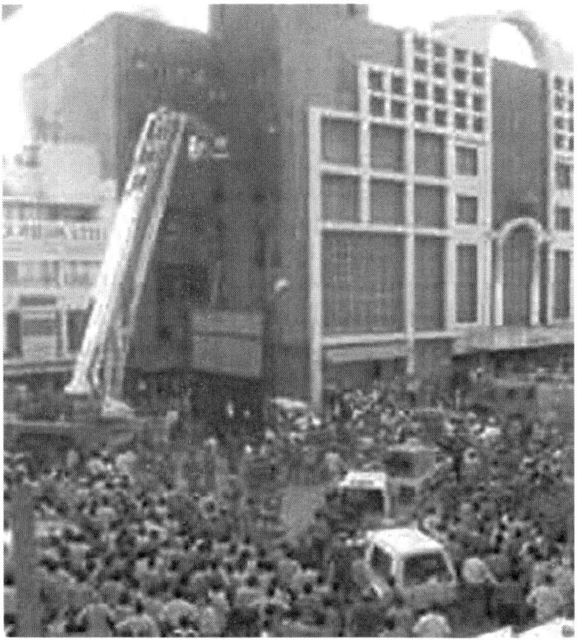

Some time back the Delhi High Court judgment awarded heavy damages for the ghastly act of negligence on account of the management of the Uphaar Cinema which had resulted in the loss of more than 50 lives and the injury of more than 100 people on 13th of June, year 1997 within the Uphaar Cinema. This judgment needs to be applauded for infusing the concept of accountability in public life.

Victims of various tragedies are generally sent back to the civil courts for providing the negligence and for assessment of the damages. This is a very long drawn process spread over unending years where the process itself punishes the claimant.

In the instant case the long and painful route of ordinary civil litigation has been avoided and the Constitutional Court has awarded the damages. Prior to this, the various High Courts have been routinely sending the claimants to the civil courts since disputed questions of facts are generally proved in the civil courts through the tedious procedures laid down in the Indian Evidence Act. Indeed, the Delhi High Court has risen to the occasion and given a go-by to the procedural technicalities in favour of substantial justice.

But this can maximum be a temporary measure. Ultimately, the Legislature will have to intervene and legislate a fundamental right to compensation in order to make institutions performing public duties accountable. As per para 6.17 of the report of the National Commission to review the working of the Constitution, it has been lamented that at present there is no law in which the principles on the basis of which misfeasance can be rendered punishable. The Commission has further opined that time has come to consider framing a law that would place responsibility on public servants for damages/compensation for patently *mala fide* actions. It has suggested that the basis for action under the proposed law could be an audit report by Commission or a body competent to examine the facts.

Giving an impetuous to the conventional law of Torts for negligence will help in curbing acts of gross negligence by various entities. For this the Court-fees should be lowered down. Right now the fee structure is highly unaffordable.

The Supreme Court has extended grant of compensation by basing it on the principle of strict liability. This means that failure to discharge public duties resulting in damages being awarded by the

Constitutional Courts like the Supreme Court and the High Courts.

In the case of *Rudul Sah* v. *State of Bihar*,[1] the right to compensation was recognized and this concept has been further been expanded in a later judgment of *Sebastian M. Hongary* v. *Union of India*,[2] whereby Rs. 1 lakh each was awarded to two women.

1. AIR 1983 SC 1086.
2. AIR 1984 SC 1026.

NEW LEGISLATION REGARDING ABORTIONS

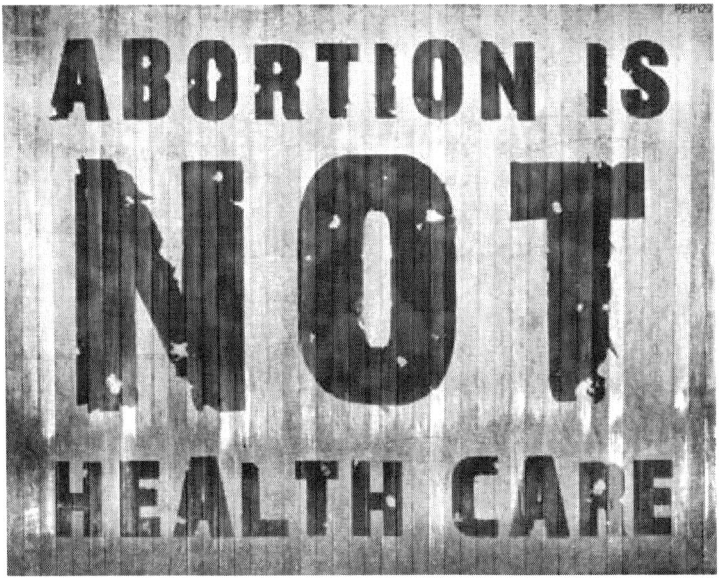

There has been a great social awakening regarding the crime against women. A new kind of spices where the girl child is killed even before the birth is now being taken care of by a highly social welfare legislation consisting of Pre-Conception and Pre-Natal Diagnostic Techniques Prohibition of Sex Selection Act, 1994 and the Medical Termination of Pregnancy Act, 1971. Because of the availability of the abortion pill – RU 486, the law relating to termination of pregnancy has been found deficient.

The medicine RU 486 does away with the requirement of surgical intervention and reduces life risks involved in the procedure for abortion. Now, with advancement of the magic pills termination of pregnancy would be possible within the privacy of ones own home without the requirement of formal hospitalization. This would greatly reduce the life threat to the woman. However, Section 4 of the Medical Termination of Pregnancy Act, 1971, lays down that there shall be no termination of pregnancy, except at a hospital established or maintained by the government or at a place which is approved by the government.

Because of Section 4, the medical practitioners would hesitate to prescribe the latest drug without proper hospitalisation, but the latest medical advances do not warrant this. The abortion could be made possible by giving this drug even at home and the lady could attend to her daily duties in a very short while. Thus, the law needs to be synchronized as per the latest situations.

The law needs to be sensitive to the new drug –RU 486 and should not be misused for gender selection and should be made available only at Government approved sale outlets after due prescription by a medical practitioner. In China, the drug is available only at approved clinics.

The Medical Termination of Pregnancy Act, 1971, has liberalized the law relating to abortions as compared to the strict British law under which abortion was a crime. This had earlier resulted in a lot many cases of women going to unauthorized practitioners for purposes of maintaining their secret. This led to many avoidable deaths. This present MTP Act has beneficially liberalized the existing law relating to termination of pregnancy.

Under Section 3 of the Act, a pregnancy may be terminated which involves a risk to life or a grave mental or physical injury to the woman. **Now, the law has been humanized to the extent that a pregnancy can also be terminated if it were likely to result in physical or mental abnormality in the child.**

As per the Amendment Act of 2002, the penal provisions for violations have been made much stricter providing for a rigorous imprisonment up to seven years. This would be a disincentive to various law breakers.

INDIA NEEDS A WITNESS PROTECTION PROGRAM

"You cannot witness for me, being slain ....
God is my witness"

William Shakespeare, Henry VI

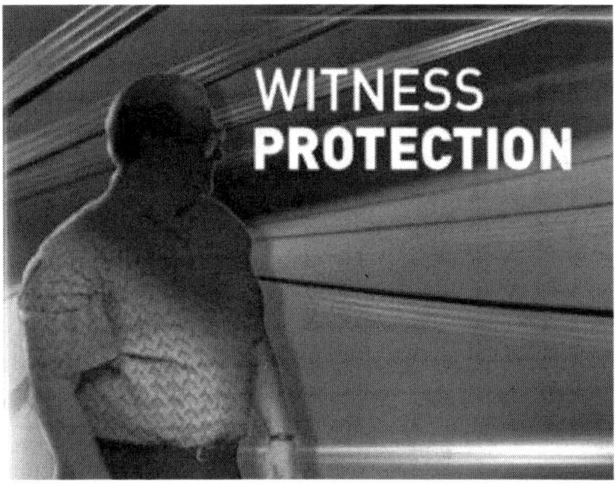

In the famous Best Bakery judgment more than twenty accused have been acquitted in charges where 14 lives had been burnt at the Best Bakery on 1st March in the year 2002. Our Countries system of dispensing criminal justice has been under great strain due to certain infamous cases. In the instant trial forty-one of the 74 witnesses examined turned hostile and the all important witness, Zaheera Sheikh, owned up in public statements appearing in the media that she resiled in the trial from her previous statements because of threats to her life. The Malimath Committee on judicial reforms had rightly recommended adoption of a witness protection program. Making the witnesses feel secure is an important responsibility of India's criminal justice system. Only then will the truth come out during the long and arduous trials.

Coming to the *Best Bakery* case[1], the trial Court Judge Additional District and Session, Judge H.U. Mahida, admitted that he was helpless as lack of sufficient evidence made acquittal the only possible verdict. Noted jurist F.S.Nariman had condemned the investigating agency for "shoddy investigation" into the case.

There is a need for soul searching by all of us. Many a time the common man feels that the courts should be more aggressive in their approach to ensure that the witnesses are not put under any kind of pressure and the truth is not put under the rug. India cannot afford to allow dilution of justice in even an ordinary case, what to speak of a case of heinous crime of national magnitude. **Stretching the principle of proof beyond reasonable doubt to certain unwarranted limits can prove counter productive in giving justice.**

What is required today is adopting an innovative and robust judicial approach in delivering justice. The court must insure that the technicalities of law give way in favour of substantial justice. The Malimath Committee rightly suggested that a provision be made in the Code of Criminal Procedure that "the quest for truth shall be the fundamental duty of every court".

Coining a witness protection program will go a long way in avoiding a key witness from turning hostile. In the United States, the witness protection program has been used for the benefit of about 23,000 persons. Recently, Canada gave protection cover to a woman who was a witness in a high profile criminal case.

This program involves giving a threatened person a new name, even new looks, along with new identity papers such as birth certificates, etc. for purposes to protect them.

---

1. *Zahira Habibulla Sheikh* v. *State of Gujarat,* AIR 2004 SC 3114: (2004) 4 SCC 158.

THE TREND OF WITNESSES TURNING HOSTILE IN CRIMINAL CASES NEEDS TO BE CURBED

"One eye Witness is better than ten hearsays".

Thomas Fuller (1654-1734)

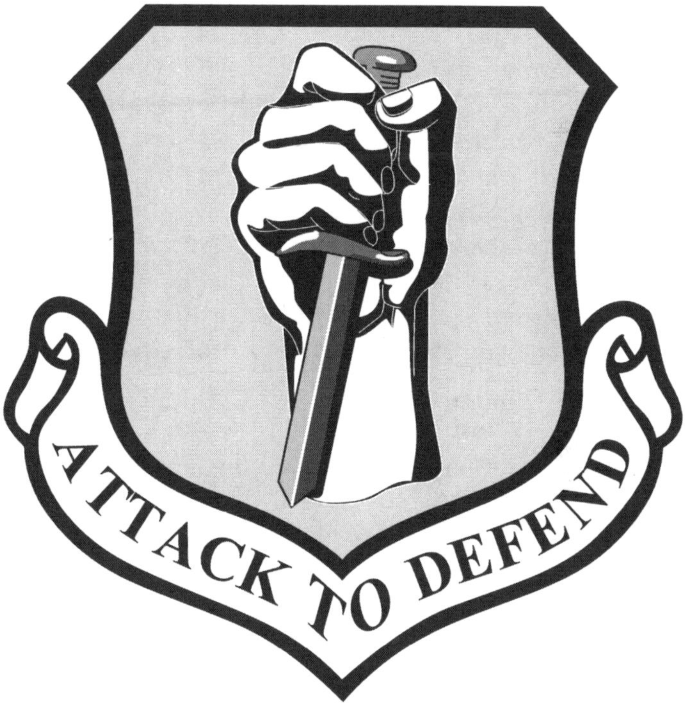

We have seeing a trend of witnesses in criminal cases increasingly succumbing to pressure tactics of the opposite side and turning hostile in court during the evidence recording proceedings. The Law Commission of India has also shown serious concern for this disturbing phenomenon and has started to focus on the grey area of witness protection. A witness protection programme involves giving the threatened person a new identity including name and even looks, if so required. This would protect a witness from intimidation meant to secure an acquittal.

Witness protection is a system that is widely being used at the International Criminal Tribunal for Rwanda. This is being used in cases of genocide for insulation of witnesses due to fears of reprisals. In Italy, only witnesses testifying in mafia related cases come under the witness protection programme. Anglo-Saxon Systems, more particularly the American and British legal systems cater to the legal protection mechanisms. In International Law, Article 40 of the United Nation Convention on the Rights of the Child suggest that children and juveniles appearing as witnesses should receive protective treatment. In addition, Article 68 of the Rome Statute states that the age of the witnesses is to be taken into account in determining appropriate protective measures.

However, India does not have any statutory law specifically laying down a witness protection programme. The Malimath Committee on Criminal Justice reforms has suggested the requirement of legislating a comprehensive law for protection of witnesses and his family. The committee further suggested that sometimes holding of 'in-camera' proceedings may be sufficient to protect the interests of the witness and at other times keeping the identity of the witness a secret would suffice.

In India, a law could be enacted providing for witness protection in specific category of cases, for example, in cases of a child witness, in cases involving sexual offences and in situations of organized and terrorist crimes. In certain European countries members of the security forces have been permitted to give evidence from behind screens. In India, giving witness through video conferencing, could also be considered. In addition, the concept of E-filing could also be used to the advantage of the threatened witnesses whereby they could be allowed to give their evidence through affidavits duly attested and signed through the usage of digital signatures. Digital signatures have been granted legal sanctity by the Information and Technology Act of India.

RAPE LAW NEEDS UPDATING AND PEOPLE NEED TO BE SENSITIZED

"Woman was and is condemned to a system under which the lawful rapes exceed the unlawful ones – a million to one".

Margaret Sanger (American Political Activist)

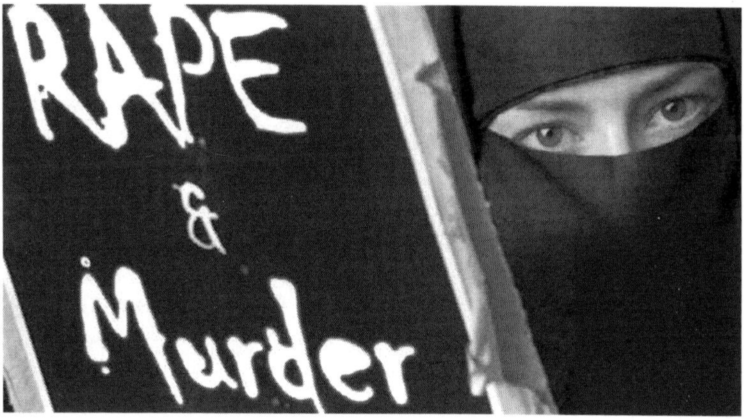

The memories are still vivid in the mind when one of a college student was gang-raped by the Presidents' Bodyguard. The latest report of National Crime Record Bureau shows a steady increase of 6.6 per cent. in the rape incidence during the period 1998 to 2000.

A recent survey of undertials at Tihar Jail revealed that majority of the rapists were serial offenders and were caught on an average after the tenth time after committing the crime. Dr. Mitras' research shows that the rapist usually becomes over confident between his fifth and tenth crime.

Sakshi, a leading women's NGO has filed a public interest petition seeking that the offence of rape defined under Section 375 of the IPC should be interpreted to include all other forms of forcible penetration including anal and oral. The legislature would do well by enacting a law prescribing adequate punishment for sexual crimes. Any new law should also cover the crime of homosexual rape and treat it with equal seriousness.

What our jurists have to understand is that what really acts as a deterrent is the certainity of conviction and not so much the quantum of punishment to be imposed. The Malimath Committee on Criminal Justice Reforms has recently recommended the sentence of life imprisonment without commutation or remission in rape convictions.

It is also very important that a particular time limit for disposing of rape cases should be laid down. Special courts with stipulated deadlines for case disposals can be setup. The investigatory process for sexual offences also needs to be expedited. Strict action needs to be prescribed to ensure compliance and on the part of the investigating machinery. Presently, investigation and adjudication taken such a long time that the slow progress of the process itself punishes the victim all over again.

In Bangladesh, Prevention of Atrocities Against Women and Children Act 18 of 1995 has been enacted. It provides that investigation and trial of rape cases should be completed within 90 days. The Malimath Committee has vary aptly recommended that a suitable provision be made requiring the investigating agency to complete the investigation within a prescribed time and for the court to dispose cases of sexual offences on priority basis within a period of four months. The citizens also need to be sensitized to the crimes which ultimately lead to the debacle of the heinous crime of rape. Public opinion in such matters proves very decisive because laws have their own limitations. It is the will of the people which gives strength to legislation.

LET US FOLLOW THE EXAMPLE OF THE CRIME FREE VILLAGE

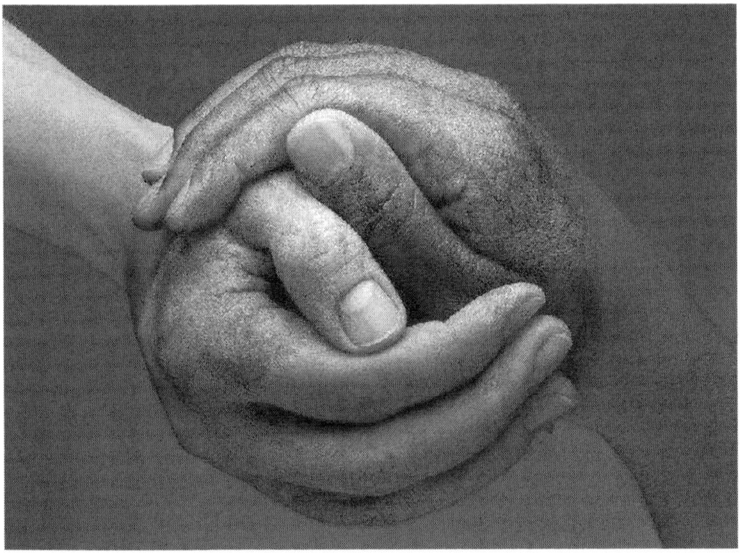

South India made us proud by having a crime free village in these modern times with no criminal case pending. This is a major achievement in view of the huge volume of pending criminal cases which has assumed the proportions of a major docket crisis in the country.

As per a study quoted in the book, 'Count Your Chickens Before They Hatch' by Arindam Chaudhri, it has been estimated that at the pace at which our court cases are resolved, it will take another 324 years only to dispose of the backlog.

The government is involved in more than 60 per cent. of all civil suit appeals. The success rate is often as low as 5 to 6 per cent.

Keeping this serious national crisis in view, the southern village has achieved wonders by attaining the zero level criminal litigation benchmark. Arindam

Chaudhri in his book comes out with a solution to achieve the national zero level litigation pendency. He writes:

"To finish this problem of criminalisation and moral bankruptcy from its root, we need to see to it that the judicial machinery starts working efficiently and, ideally speaking, we don't have too much time for that. We should try to solve it in next five years itself.

"Our research points out that for this we need to allocate Rs. 3,600 crore per year over the next five years for employing on emergency services and short service commission, practicing lawyers with years of experience to act as Judges (45,000 additional judges on the basis of Rs. 4 lakh per judge with supporting staff, etc.) to clear backlog, in the next five years. Later, as the backlog comes down, these judges would be crucial in keeping up the fast pace of the judicial system. This will reduce criminalisation of the civil life enormously and bring back values into our lives and our work."

People in the driving seat should give practical shape to Chaudhri's conclusions if we are to achieve the presidential vision of an ideal and vibrant India by the year 2020.

One is reminded of Justice Learned Hand's remark: "As a litigant, I should dread a lawsult beyond almost anything else, short of sickness and death."

How rightly has the eminent jurist late **Nani A. Palkhivala** in his book, **'We, the Nation,'** pointed out: **"If I were asked to mention the greatest drawback of the administration of justice in India today, I would say that it is delay. There are Inordiate delays in the disposal of cases. We, as a nation, have some fine qualities, but a sense of the value of time is not one of them. Perhaps there are historical reasons for our relaxed attitude to time. Ancient India had evolved the** concepts of eternity and infinity. So what do 30 years wasted in a litigation matter against the backdrop of eternity? We in India believe in the theory of rebirth and therefore many can believe that they will take birth again and again to see the victory of their legal battles."

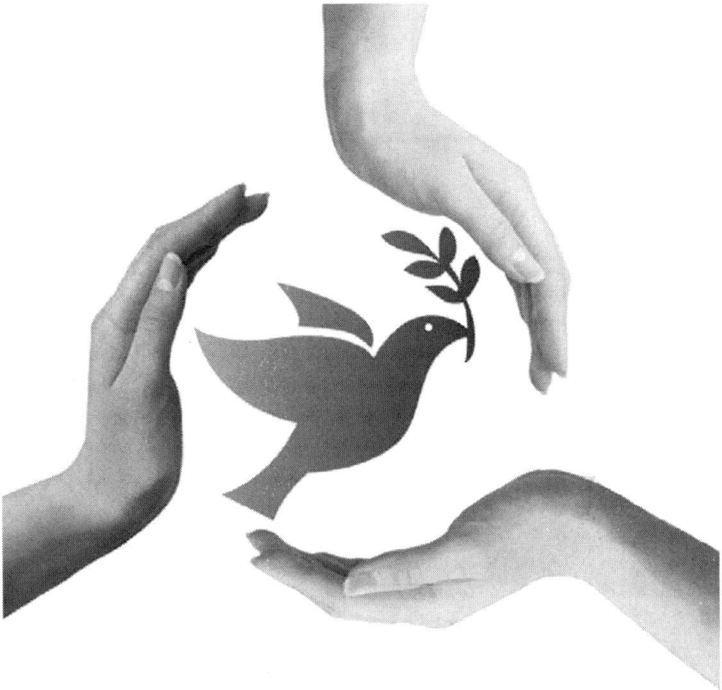

LET US TAKING A FRESH LOOK AT JAILS – THE BACKYARD OF OUR COUNTRY

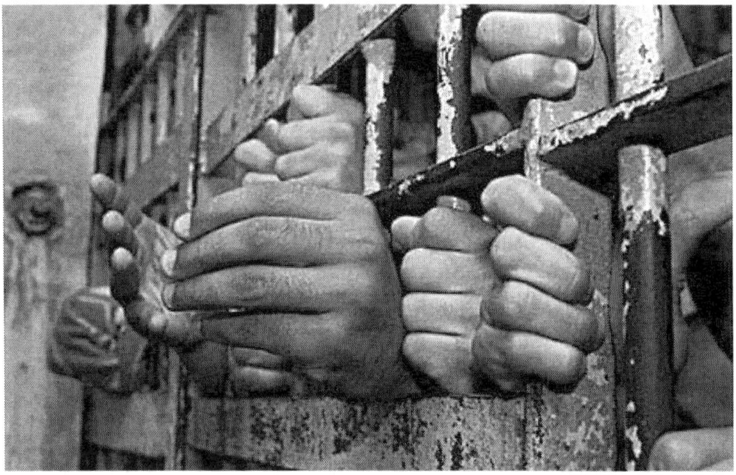

Various quarters have been crying hoarse for jail reforms. **Jails are the backyard of a country and there also the Bench mark of the nations human face.** The noted jurist justice Krishna Iyer in a string of judgments including that of the famous *Sunil Batra's* case has lamented on the pitable plight of jail inmates. In November 1999, the Chief Justice of India had written to Chief Justice's of all High Courts about the pitiable plight of under trial prisoners languishing in jails and prison inmates. The Supreme Court in the case *Common Cause* v. *Union of India*,[1] and in other judgments had issued directions for release on bail and discharge of certain categories of under-trials. Notwithstanding the fact the highest court in the country has been issuing directions for improving the plight of jail inmates and even

1. 1996 (4) SCC 775.

releasing some of them there has been overcrowding of more than 30% in the jails against the built in capacity. More than 70% of the jail populations constitutes the under trial. This is leading to all kinds of avoidable complications within the precincts of the jails. The National Human Rights Commission has lamented that despite several judicial pronouncements on the subject, under-trials are still languishing in large numbers as 'forgotten souls' who continue to suffer hardships of confinement although their guilt was yet to be established. Another organizational blunder of prison administration was the housing of hardened criminals along with small-time convicts. This could result in a breeding ground for hardcore criminals. Arindham Chaudhari in his book 'The Great Indian Dream' describes the prisoners in jails as divided into two classes – 'the haves' and 'the have-nots'. Somewhere down the line, the national objective of imprisonment being not only punitive but also reformative seems to have been lost sight of. It is our constitutional mandate to make efforts to turn an offender into a non-offender. In the given scenario, special emphasis needs to be laid on decongesting the jail conditions and providing a decent standard of daily living, including basic amenities and hygienic conditions. It is necessary to periodically review the cases of under-trials and to release on personal bonds, the offenders who cannot arrange for sureties. Doctor Kiran Bedi has done remarkable work in Tihar Jail when she was incharge of the prisons. She successfully created a congenial environment for the growth of the condemned lot. Taking cue from her example, our institutions like the government need to be more sensitised to those locked behind the jail doors.

PLEA-BARGAINING IS AN EFFECTIVE TOOL FOR SPEEDING UP JUSTICE

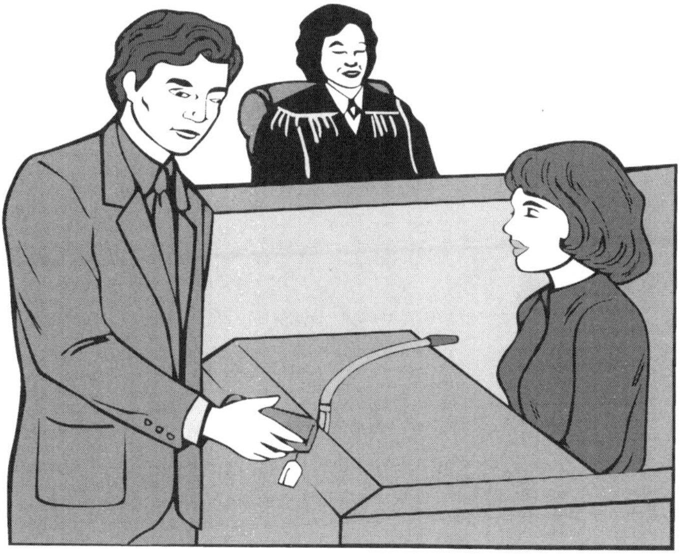

A Chennai Fast Track Court Judge, Mr. K. Ashokan had created a record of sorts by pronouncing a judgment in a span of just 44 days. **Really, the justice in slow motion which has changed tracks and gone over to the fast track is an appreciable achievement requiring commendation from all quarters. This is like injecting a lethargic person into hyper activity.** Of late, the docket crisis had reached such enormous proportions that many a litigant has felt that the slow pace of justice delivery had become so exacting that it has started punishing both the winner as well as the loser. In this background, this 44 days verdict came as a breath of fresh air with a message of optimism. Judge Ashokan has gone down in history by sentencing four men to seven years imprisonment for killing a man in a drunken brawl.

However, unfortunately the very establishment of fast track courts had run into trouble for lack of funds. To sustain this life-infusing institution, the Supreme Court had to go in for crisis intervention by extending the tenure of fast track courts. The Apex Court had to approach the Centre for arranging funds to enable the fast track institution to survive. **It is time that the nation thinks in terms of according financial independence to the judiciary in order to make its independence more meaningful.**

However, the Central Government as well exhibited its *bona fides* and well meaning intensions by going in for fast tracing measures like introduction of the concept of plea-bargaining in the criminal justice system.

Plea-bargaining is essentially a negotiated settlement where the defendant agrees to plead guilt in exchange for certain concessions from the prosecution. Plea-bargaining on the US model has gained acceptability the world over because it has been the experience of many a countries that as such as even 90 per cent. of convictions come from negotiated pleas leaving at times less than 10 per cent. of the criminal cases resulting in a full fledged trial. **Italy has gone far enough to pass a federal legislation formally legalizing it.** During the past generation, plea-bargaining has steadily crept into many European countries' systems. It has been a common experience that crowded calendars and overburdened prisons provide powerful incentives to many judges and prosecutors for the plea-bargaining concept. India has done well by tuning in to this time tested tool of plea-bargaining.

INJECT NATIONAL INSTITUTIONS WITH THE SERUM OF TRUTH

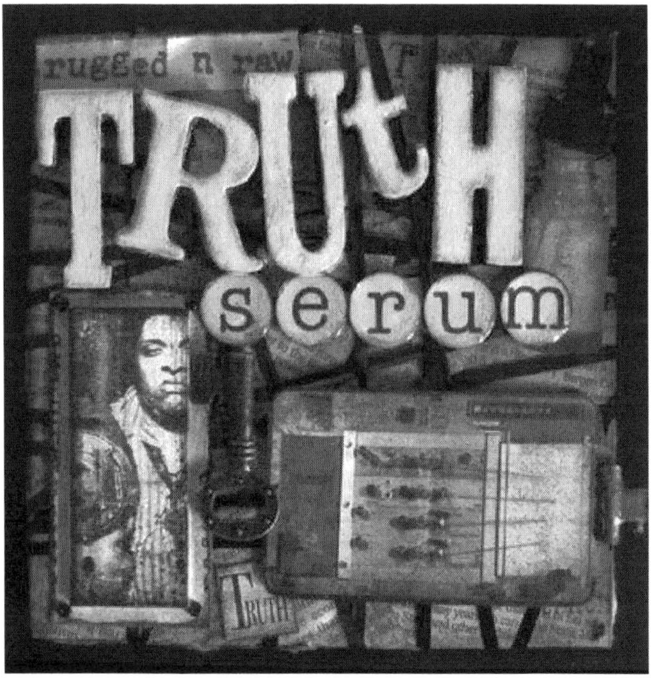

The story of Indian Judicial system is becoming a story punctuated by many hostile witnesses during the course of trial. We have seen this in the case of best bakery and other land mark trials. This disturbing phenomena dilutes the prevalence of truth during the proceedings. Keeping this in mind the legislature has introduced the US concept of plea-bargaining by amending the CrPC. It is high time that the nation wakes up to falsehood practiced by witnesses and addresses the issue of rising witness hostility.

Time is now ripe for the proverbial Goddess of justice to remove the symbolic bandage from her eyes to distinguish between truth and falsehood. Sifting truth from deceit like separating grain from the chaff poses a major challenge to the judicial system of today. **One of the proposed amendments is to make a witness, who retracts from a statement before a magistrate under Section 164 of the CrPC, run the high risk of inviting perjury charges.** The judge ought to issue a 'Miranda-warning' to the witness being held for perjury.

Even the Malimath Committee had recommended amendments in the Criminal Code for making the 'quest for the truth' a fundamental duty of every court. Malimath's report begins with the regret in the words of **"Lies and falsehood practiced under an oath of truth are cruel but curable."** The symptoms and not the disease have been treated. Yet, Malimath has done well by proposing an amendment in Section 344 of the Cr PC to enhance the sentence for false evidence from the present three months to two years imprisonment.

Enlarging the scope and power of courts under Sections 311 and 482 of the CrPC to enable the courts to make appropriate orders necessary for discovering the truth is overdue. Inherent powers of the High Court under Section 482, if given more teeth, can go a long way in establishing truth in proceedings. Presently, the procedure for taking action against perjury is cumbersome and impracticable. Courts would be well advised to insist on "summary procedure" under Section 344 of the CrPC for trial of false evidence offences.

Indeed, **Benjamin Disraeli**, the 19th century British Prime Minister, was correct when he remarked that **"justice was truth in action." In fact, had it not been for truth and justice, the Crown would have inevitably gone to the persons with the longest sticks and the readiest fists.** The inevitability of victory of justice has been reiterated by many a thinkers, including **Thomas Middleton**, who expressed his belief in the ultimate prevalence of justice. Judicial history, dating back about two centuries ago, reminds us of Edmund Burke's remarks made in the British Parliament thus: "It is the duty of the judge to receive every offer of evidence, apparent material, suggested to him, though the parties themselves through negligence, ignorance or corrupt collusion should not bring it forward. A judge is not placed in that high situation merely as a passive instrument of parties. He has a duty of his own, independent of them, which is to investigate truth."

Institutions have to be strengthened by having truth as a high priority on the national agenda. No doubt our national motto of 'Satyameva Jayate' voices our national sentiment, but it needs to be given a further fillip by imbibing the ethos of truth in our judicial institutions.

LAW GRAPPLES WITH ISSUES LIKE SEX DETERMINATION

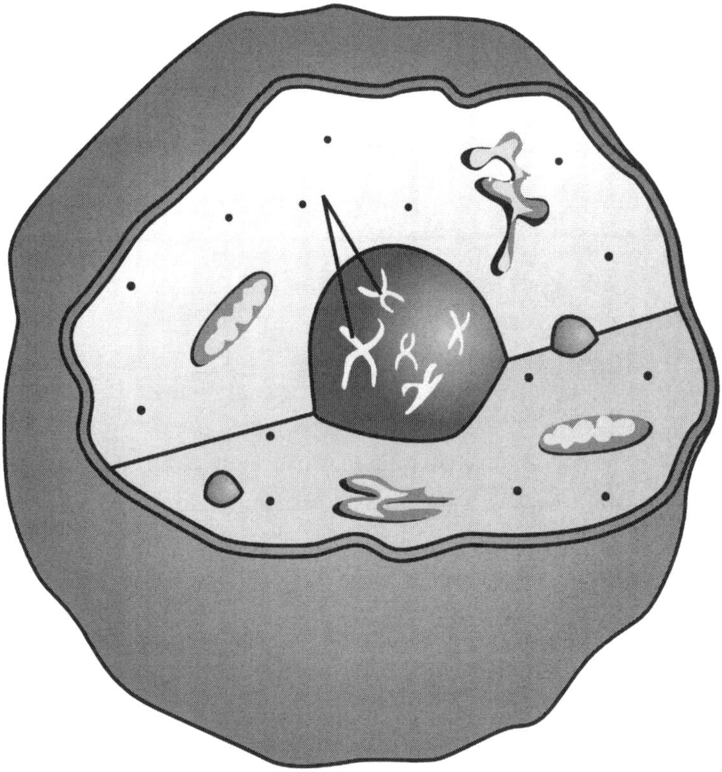

All life is precious. Historically this has been indicated by great emperors like Ashoka who went to the extent of even preserving the life of animals by establishing hospitals for these living creatures. In this great historical back ground of preserving life, the law is catching up to keep the sanctity of the human fetus intact.

Female foetuses are being nipped in the bud. Lakhs of girls are being eliminated prior to birth due to foetal sexing in our country. Sex selection hits at the roots of gender justice. 'In the sexual harassment case of *Vishaka* v. *State of Rajasthan*, AIR 1997 SC 3011, the Supreme Court has reiterated the fundamental right of Gender Equality and 'Right to Life'. The Pre-conception and Pre-Natal Diagnostic Techniques (Prohibition of Sex Selection) Act, 1994 and the Medical Termination of Pregnancy Act, 1971 are bold initiatives to counter the cult of 'baby-boys to order'. The international medical journal 'Lancet' has aptly remarked, "new technologies have the potential to create new problems for society". Till 1981, for 100 years, child sex ratios in Punjab were around 900 girls per 1000 boys. In a larger perspective, though the international population conference at Cairo gave the attitude to informed and responsible persons to make free reproductive decisions regarding family needs, certain countries like Hong Kong, United Kingdom and parts of Australia prohibit 'sex selection' for family balancing.

In India, the 'boy syndrome' is more due to religious and economic considerations. Incidentally, it is the same country where on September 4, 1987 18 year-old Roop Kanwar was burnt alive in the pyre of her husband. This was followed by another incident of *sati* in 2002 at a Madhya Pradesh village. Incidentally, 2002 marked 173 years since Lord Willam Bentinck outlawed *sati* practice. These incidents are taking place despite India being a signatory to both the UN Charter on Human Rights and Declaration on Women. It's also a 'wake-up call' for National Commission on Women. With the PNDT and MTP enactments, female sexing is now both legal as well as moral issue.

Thus, Section 6 of the PNDT Act has made a bold effort by restraining the heartless by banning diagnostic techniques for determining the sex of the foetus. To make the vision of the PNDT Act a living reality, Section 7 has been incorporated which provides for setting up of

Central Supervisory Board comprising high officials and experts. The human face of the enactment is reflected in Section 4, which provides for exceptions to the ban in cases of chromosomal abnormalities, genetic diseases and congenital anomalies. The deterrent aspect is contained in Section 27, which makes every offence under the Act as cognizable, non-bailable and non-compoundable. However, Rule 9 and certain other provisions provide for maintenance of records. A word of caution: During implementation of the law, over emphasis on documentation and paper work may dilute the quality and role of medical professionals. Regarding the related legislation of pregnancy termination, Section 4 of the MTP Act 1971 bans termination of pregnancy except in a hospital or in an approved institution. It is time we have faith in the female tryst of destiny with life.

TIME FOR LAW TO CATER FOR THE NEGLECTED CHILD

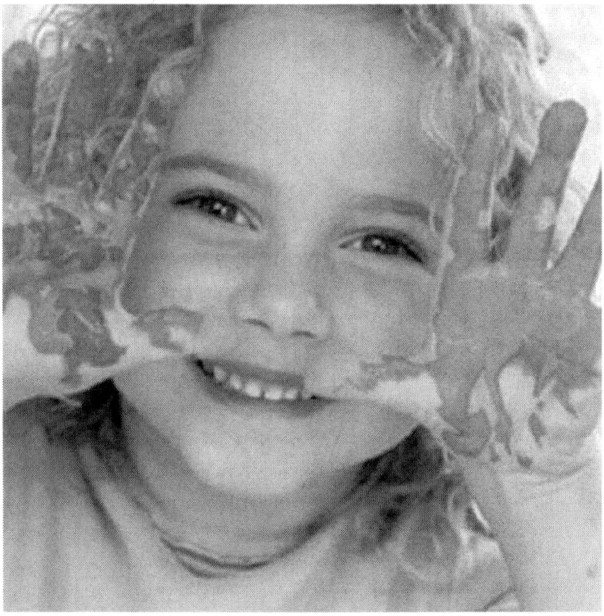

Since time immemorial the child has been a subject of exploitation by unscrupulous elements of society. The memory of the tragic episode with children at Nithari is still fresh in our minds. Unfortunately it took twenty month to even register FIRs of the missing children at Nithari.

Surely, we are not to believe that existing laws are inadequate to even register an FIR in cases of missing children. Though Section 154 of the Code of Criminal Procedure definitely needs a re-reading, it clearly says that a police officer incharge of a police station shall reduce all information, related to a cognizable offence, in writing. Are we as a nation being led further to believe that the Nithari offences are non-cognisable? Justice Leela Seth was far more palatable when she dubbed the delay as a clear dereliction of duty.

King Martin Luther had once rightly remarked that: **"The ultimate tragedy in life is not the brutality of the bad, but the silence of the good".** Though Article 32 of the United Nations Convention on the Rights of Child recognizes the child's right to be protected, Indian Laws and their implementation are grossly out of tune with International mandates. Operating within the limitation of inadequate statutory law, the courts have started focusing on this neglected area: that is a child without a childhood. The Supreme Court's observation in the *Rosy Jacob* v. *Jacob* case that children were neither mere chattel nor mere playthings is relevant at this point.

Further in the case of *Bandhua Mukti Morcha* v. *Union of India*,[1] the court emphasized that the child's Right to Life under Article 21 included the Right to Dignity and the Right against Abuse. The Supreme Court has categorically laid down in the *State of Punjab* v. *Mahinder Singh Chawla*,[2] that the Right to Life includes the Right to Health also.

Depriving the child of his childhood is a national stigma, which prompted present Union Home Minister P. Chidambram to observe in his write up in a National Daily on November 10, 2002, that it was a pity that governments, which proclaimed their concern for abandoned cattle (even dead cattle), had no concern for street children. He thought that certain other things could wait till we were able to provide for thousands of street children.

As a consequence of the Nithari serial killings, the Union Government has constituted a committee to look into the issue of child protection. The bureaucratic top-heavy committee needs to be more representative in character for effective delivery. Noida incident being the basic reference point of the committee, its agenda needs to be broadened so as to cover child abuse in general. The

---

1. AIR 1984 SC 802.
2. AIR 1997 SC 1225.

government has been contemplating a new law – 'Offences Against Children Act, 2007'. It would do well to make inbuilt pre-emptive measures an integral part of the new law so as to ensure that no child like flower is nipped in the bud. If the contemplated law is not to be compared to a stillborn child, it must ensure that its wide sweep covers all contingencies including those of human perversion. Then whether it's children being exploited like those making carpets in Uttranchal, sifting tendu leaves in Orissa, rolling 'beedies' and making matchsticks down South, they need to be sheltered. How right is the remark 'Child and God are where they are celebrated'. **Nobel laureate Gabrial Mistral** had forcefully lamented and appealed to the society to pay attention to the most important and oft neglected backbone of society, *i.e.* the child. He said: **"We are guilty of many errors and faults, but our worst crime is abandoning the children, neglecting the foundation of life. Many of the things we need can wait – the child cannot. Right now is the time his bones are being formed, his blood is being made and his senses are being developed. To him we cannot answer "Tomorrow", his name is 'Today'."** Thus, law has to catch up with child, who is the proverbial father of man.

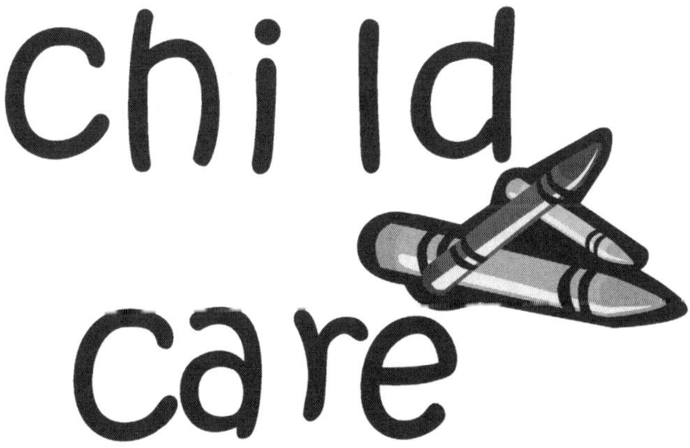

BALANCING PRIVACY AND RIGHTS UNDER R.T.I. ACT

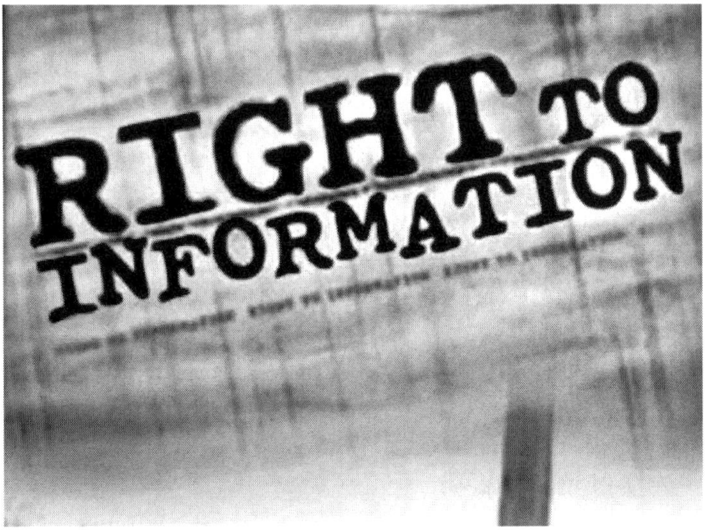

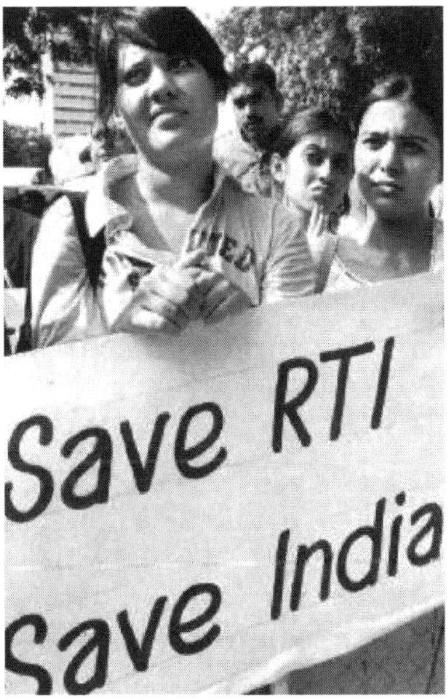

It has been a time felt need that our police system should be improved in terms of technology in order to keep pace with crime detections for our fast converting digital economy. **Hess had said that a modern thief could steal more with a computer than with a gun.** Even Alvin Toffler, while writing his monumental book 'Future Shock', must have anticipated **that tomorrow's terrorists may be able to do more damage with a keyboard than with a bomb.**

Many a statesmen have been regularly warning that the neglected areas of justice and crime need our pressing attention. Under the present laws, the jurisdiction would correspond to the place of committal and to damage occurrence of a crime with often both locations overlapping. But **in the digital world, the crime could well orginate overseas and could damage digital organizational weath in multiple locations.**

A study by McConnel International, a Washington-based consulting company, revealed that 33 of the 52 nations surveyed had not updated their Criminal Codes to deal with cyber offences. The US laws covered nine out of 10 crimes. Philippines was the only exception to have covered all types of crimes. **Cyber crimes could well be data related, including interception, modification and theft; network tampering, virus distribution, computer fraud and forgery.**

The Andhra Pradesh High Court judicially adjudicated the advent of cyber crime in India in the case of *Meena Degala,* 2005 (1) RCR (Cr) 434. Though India has enacted the Information and Technology Act, 2000, which provides for a regulatory environment for electronic commerce, it has been found inadequate on many counts. **Unlike the United States and European countries, India is yet to enact a separate legislation on privacy.** Though Section 72 of the IT Act deals with privacy punishment of up to two years imprisonment, this section deals only with the disclosure of confidential information and not with interception. Privacy, as a separate legal concept, dates back to an essay published in 1890. With the Right to Information Act in its infancy in India, the real challenge would be to balance the conflict points between the public's right to information and the individual's right to privacy. The U.S. Supreme Court, in the case of *'Department of Justice* v. *Reporters' Committee for Freedom of Press,* 440 US 949 (1979)', involving information requests from the media for records known as 'rap sheets' maintained by the FBI, had decided that disclosure would be an invasion of privacy under the Freedom of Information Act. It is time that India does the sensitive and delicate tight rope balancing between individual privacy and the publics' right to information under the R.T.I. Act.

ACCOUNTABILITY @ CONSTITUTIONAL TORT

(A Concept for Disaster Prevention)

"I repeat . . . . that all power is a trust – that we are accountable for its exercise – that, from the people, and for the people, all springs, and all must exist."

Benjamin Disraeli

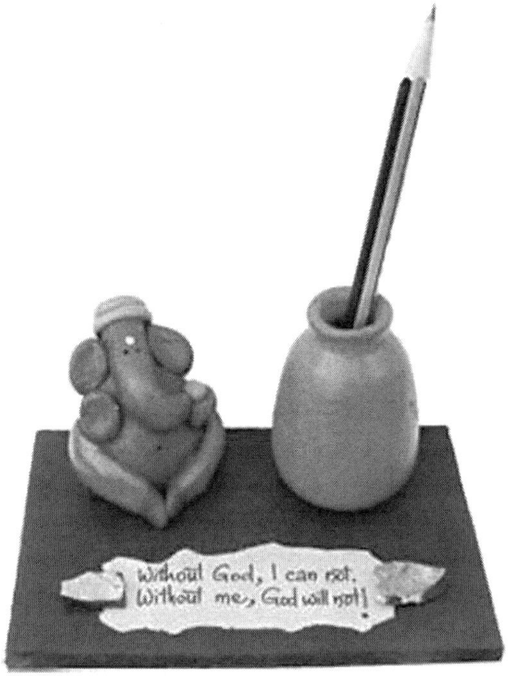

Seeing Living examples of prosperity like Japan, China, and Singapore, one wonders where we in India have gone wrong. After great introspection, the answer is, that there is a total lack of accountability in our systems. We have proved unworthy of the shield of security provided to our governmental functionaries. The general attitude is "CHALTA HAI" (IT REALLY DOES NOT MATTER) and MERA KYA BIGAD LOGAYE (Do whatever you can – None can harm me). The genesis of the rot of our system is traceable to the mis-governance and inefficiency of public institutions due to lack of accountability. There is too much government but too little administration; Under trials have languished in jails for periods more than the actual sentences for the offences charged. One is reminded of the decades old Shakespearean dilemma depicted in the work "The rape of Lucrece" in the words:

"The patient dies while the physian sleeps;

The orphan pines while the oppressor feeds;

Justice is feasting while the widow weeps"

Recent example of **unarmed helpless citizens demanding clean drinking water in Bombay being mercilessly beaten and one of them losing his life for water is a slur on the Indian System and an example the agony a citizen has to undergo for the mere procurement of drinking water. One is reminded of the famous remark of a visionary. "Water, water, everywhere not a drop to drink."** There have been judicially noticed examples in cases like *Khatri* v. *State of Bihar* where prisoners have been blinded. Thus accountability is a major national issue with us. **Rightly has it been remarked that an hour of justice is worth a hundred of prayers.**

To me, the sole answer lies in reviving the shelved "Government (Liability in Torts) Bill" which was introduced in Parliament way back- in the year 1967 and has yet to see the light of the day. Even countries like England which believe in the maxim that the "King can do no Wrong", finally responded to the prevailing situation by the introducing the Crown Proceedings Act in the year 1947. With this law, the King who could earlier not be sued for tortuous liability for wrong committed by its servants during the course of employment was now made liable for torts committed by them like a private individual.

The broad framework of the language of Constituional Tort could be as follows:—

Constitutional Tort shall include Constitutional and Statutory violations and illegal omissions by any Constitutional or Governmental functionary or anyone acting under them and shall include their agents who shall be accountable for the discharge or implementation of a law for the time being in force connected directly or indirectly with a public function. The commission or illegal omission shall be culpable under the criminal law and redressible with Examplary compensatory damages.

The Constituitonal Tort is proposed to be a specific and a speedy right entitling its seeker Directions/Fiats/ Mandates Directly from Constitutional Courts consisiting of the Supreme Courts and High Courts.

The conventional law of torts has not developed in India due to heavy court fees involved and red tapism of systems. Thus, there is a total lack of any effective accountabilty law. The R.T.I. is yet in its infancy and grappling with many initial obstacles.

Non implementation of many of the existing laws could be an important component of Constitutional Tort. The bane of India is that there are to many laws and too less of justice as the noted jurist N.A. Palkiwala put it. Having a law on the statute book and not implementing it is a total mockery and a sham. Restoring the credibilty of the system can be only by purging it from daily instances of injustice being faced by the common man. Rightly it has been remarked thus:—

"Justice being taken away, then, what are kingdoms but great robberies? For what are robberies themselves, but litte kingdoms?"

The winds of change have also engulfed America which has introduced the Federal Torts Claims Act, 1946. This Act lays down the broad principles which decide the issues related to State Liability in cases of default.

Unfortunately, we in India have no specific legislation which governs the liability of the State for the torts committed by its functionaries during the course of their employment. However, the Constitution embodies Article 300 which touches upon the liability of the Union or the State in tortuous acts of the government in a peripheral way. The fallout of this article which can the traced to the Government of India Act of 1935, 1915 and 1858 is that the liability of the government would be the same as that of EAST INDIA COMPANY before 1858.

Since quite some time, judicial pronouncements on questions of State liability have been distinguishing between sovereign and Non – Sovereign and Non-Sovereign functions of the State. The uncertainty on the issue was sought to be remedied by the Law Commission in its First Report Commission in 1956 which highlighted the need for a comprehensive legislation for fixing tortuous Liability of the government towards third parties for wrong of its servants and agents during the course of employment . Based on the Law Commission report, the government (Liability in Torts) Bill was presented in the Indian Parliament way - back in the year 1967. It has yet to become law. Even, more dismal is the situation in which many of the laws already in existence are not being implemented. We as a nation need to re-think as to whether non-Implementation of Expert Commission Reports and Non-Implementation of existing laws should also be made actionable under the Law of Tort?

Law of Torts covers actions for damages for legal injuries which infringes upon rights to personal security, reputation and property. Derived from a French word

"Tort" which comes from 'Tortem' implying a twisted or a crooked act. Tortuous Liability arises from the breach of a legal duty and is redressible by an action for unliquindated damages where the amount is not predetermined and is dependant upon the discretion of the court. The law of Torts is a part of the Common Law. In the Union of India (1988 MPLJ 540) "It has also been held that Section 9 of the Code of Civil Procedure, which enables a Civil Court to try all suits of a civil nature, impliedly confers jurisdiction to apply the law of Torts as principles of justice, equity and good conscience.

"Lord Scarman has aptly remarked in the context of the law of Torts thus:

> " The Common Law, which in constitutional context means judicially developed equity, covers everything which is not covered by statutes ... the function of the court is to decide the case before it, even though the decision may require the extension or adaptation of a principle or in some cases the creation of a new law to meet the justice of the case . . ."

In *Devakinandan's* case, the Supreme Court culled out an accountability landmark concept of Constitutional Tort and Compensatory Jurisprudence. The court awarded Rs. 25,000 as exemplary costs for harassing the petitioner who had been dragged to court for twelve long years to get his pension.

Further, in the case of *Rudul Sah* under Article 32, the Court awarded monetary compensation for illegal detention resulting in violation of a Fundamental Right. The concept of Sovereign Immunity was put in the background and a concept of civil liability arising due to violation of personal liberty was judicially recognized. However, we have a long way to go in giving it a Constitutional and Statutory status with functional efficiency. The proposition of Constitutional Tort was given further impetus by the Supreme Court in the cases if *Saheli* v. *Commissioner of Police* and *Nilabati Behera* v. *State of Orissa,* followed by many more rulings.

However, Judicial verdicts have their limitations and proper accountability in the various systems can only be restored by legislating the concept of Constitutional Tort and giving it an exhaustive and proper functionally effective shape. Only then, will the daily trials and sufferings of the common man be mitigated. As of now, there an epidemic of national complacency, inefficiency and 'couldn't care-less approach'. There is rampant pollution and adulteration in medicines, eatables, water and even the air we breathe in. Is this not slow poisoning? No wonder, instances of cancer have become as common as flu. It could well be anybody's turn. After 63 years of independence, there is a dearth of the very basics like electricity, water and infrastructure. The sooner , the tool of Constitutional Tort is brought in -, the better it is. ***Let us experiment with the new. How correct was Justice James Pickles, when he aptly remarked as far back as in 1987 thus: 'While tradition is the essence of common law, we should not be ruled by the dead'.***

V.R. Krishna Iyer
(Former Judge, Supreme Court)

Fax and Phone : 0484 – 2370088
"SATGAMAYA"
M.G. ROAD, ERNAKULAM
KOCHI - 682 011
Email : satgamaya@dataone.in
Website : www.vrkrishnaiyer.org

A CRITICAL APPRECIATION

Swaraj is what we fought for and struggled to gain our independence from the imperial crown of Briton. Gandhiji, formally flattered as the Father of the Nation is no where in the leadership of India's independent progress. The Preamble to the Constitution which speaks of justice, social, economic and political is mere rhetoric and our democracy which created the Constitution by We, the People of India inscribed a Preamble which promised a tryst with destiny elaborated by the first Prime Minister Nehru where he put the highest priority on wiping the tears from every eye. Mahatma Gandhi also felt disappointed with our westernised conceptualisation of development. Gandhiji said: 'The Gandhian concept of development rejected the idea that it should aim primarily at the creation of material wealth or the satisfaction of insatiable, endlessly multiplied needs. 'Insofar as we have made the modern materialistic craze our goal,' he wrote, 'so far are we going downhill in the path of progress.' (The Third World Tomorrow)

The fundamental rights stressed in the Constitution underscored the right to life as quintessential. Human rights which cover the right to food, shelter, movement, employment and public health and education is contained in Parts III and IV. Nevertheless 60 years after Independence when we read these provisions our democracy is a travesty. Our socialism is disdained in practice by privatisation and nationalism has been superseded by globalization because our economy is controlled and shaped by trans-national corporations for whom the balance sheets are more important than the lives of masses who die of cold winter and heat wave. The right to life necessarily means life with dignity, health, education and fresh air and safe travel. Nehru put it this in his historic Tryst with Destiny speech:

> That future is not one of ease or resting but of incessant striving so that we may fulfil the pledges we have so often taken and the one we shall take today. The service of India means the service of the millions who suffer. It means the ending of poverty and ignorance and disease and inequality of opportunity. The ambition of the greatest man of our generation has been to wipe every tear from every eye. That may be beyond us, but as long as there are tears and suffering, so long our work will not be over.

Today in India everything is under imperial domain. No fresh air, no pure water, no unpolluted food and not even roads which are not subject to tolls and *de-facto* privatised. Our corporations are so powerful that they can control the White House and wipe out population by starvation. Ralph Nadar, one of the greatest fighters through Public Interest Litigation against corporate domination has said:

> Crime statistics almost wholly ignore corporate or business crime; there is no list of the ten most wanted corporations, the law affords no means of regularly collecting data on corporate crime; and much corporate criminal behaviour (such as pollution) has not been made a crime because of corporate opposition. For example, wilful and knowing violations of auto, tire, radiation, and gas pipeline safety standards are not considered crimes under the relevant statutes even if lives are lost as a result. The description of an array of corporate crimes in this forthright book reveals a legal process requiring courage, not routine duty, by officials to enforce the laws against such outrages. The law is much more comfortable sentencing a telephone coin box thief to five years than sentencing a billion-dollar price-fixing executive to six weeks in jail. In one recounting after another, the authors

pile up the evidence toward one searing conclusion—that corporate economic, product and environmental crimes dwarf other crimes in damage to health, safety and property, in confiscation or theft of other people's monies, and in control of the agencies which are supposed to stop this crime and fraud. And it all goes on year after by blue-chip corporate recidivists. Why? It is easy to answer—"power." But that is the beginning, not the end, of understanding.

.........The Third World is under a dependencia syndrome and their freedom is at the mercy of mighty corporations. **These dimensions of our slavery have been dealt with graphically and in lurid detail by the author Shri Ravi Sodhi in his scholarly work "Legal Balm". Indeed reading his book reminds me of an anonymous poem quoted in America Inc.:**

The law locks up both man and woman
Who steals the goose from off the common?
But lets the greater felon loose
Who steals the common from the goose?

.....Our politicians look to the next election which is expensive. Our statesmen who are rarest of the rare looked to the next generation. The misfortune is the Republic of India with an excellent Constitution is staggering in progress. When the Prime Minister Indira Gandhi struck down the privy purses of princes and nationalised coal and iron these were struck down by the court. When we become independent the masses were full of expectation of a transformation in favour of the poorer classes. But expectations darkened into anxiety and anxiety into dismay and dismay into despair. So much so, desperate people turn extremists and violent. Today the most common feature of our Republic is terrorism and not merely people below the poverty line but twenty crores allegedly under the hunger line.

Crimes are on the increase and law takes decades to finish. As the author points out "According to the Report of Crime in India, 2000 published by the National Crime Bureau, 49,21,710 criminal cases under the IPC were pending at the end of the year 2000. The country's experiment with the fast track courts has yet to create the necessary impact. The concept of this species of courts has not been able to deliver in many of the states. The Malimath Committee has suggested the setting up of an Arrears Eradication Scheme on similar lines of the fast track courts project. The scheme is scripted to eradicate the arrears pending within a record time of five years. It suggests the functioning of courts on part time basis with part time judges by adjustments with regular courts."

Fast track courts are counterfeit. The richer classes have their litigations by a pending legislation. The poor people have their cases heard for several years which takes a life time of judicial process in short. The three instrumentalities of the Republic are conditioned by an economic perspective pro-rich and anti-poor as pointed out by Prof. Griffith the 'The Politics of the Judiciary'. **Mr. Ravi Sodhi has produced an excellent work which needs serious attention by the builders of the Nation. I commend this book to the thinkers and statesmen of our country and more than that for a national debate.** Five-star life is a grave danger. Money more than man matters today. Our hospitals, our colleges, even our public highways are now private investments...... Gandhi is no more and Nehru forgotten. We have to have a new Law India if humanity here is to survive.......

"Who lives if India dies, who dies if India lives."

10 February, 2010

By Justice V.R. Krishna Iyer
Former Judge, Supreme Court